Planning Your Financial Future

Investments, Insurance, Wills

Planning Your Financial Future

Investments, Insurance, Wills

Joseph Newman—Directing Editor

U.S.NEWS & WORLD REPORT BOOKS

A division of U.S.News & World Report, Inc.

WASHINGTON, D.C.

Copyright © 1972
by U.S.News & World Report, Inc.
2300 N Street, N.W., Washington, D.C. 20037

First Printing, 1972
Second Printing, Revised, April, 1974
Third Printing, Revised, October, 1974
Fourth Printing, April, 1975
Fifth Printing, Revised, November, 1975
Sixth Printing, September, 1976
Seventh Printing, Revised, November, 1976

All rights reserved, including the right to reproduce this book
or portions thereof in any form.

ISBN 0-89193-401-4

Library of Congress Catalog Card Number 72-88681

Printed in the United States of America

Contents

Illustrations

CHAPTER 1

Managing
Your
Money

The American people have the reputation of being the wealthiest in the world, and this distinction is well supported by facts. The median family income in the United States now is about $14,000 a year. Over a lifetime of work, this means that the "average" American breadwinner earns a total of more than $500,000—a fortune, over a half-million dollars. Many Americans, of course, earn more. A sizeable number exceed the million-dollar mark during their working years.

Yet many of these American families are troubled by financial insecurity. Why so many sleepless nights, so much worry over money in the world's wealthiest nation?

A major reason is that Americans eat up their incomes, large or small. In pressing for a higher and higher standard of living—another car, an extra television set, a longer and more luxurious vacation in a still more distant land, they fall into a hand-to-mouth existence. Skill in managing money has not kept pace with the increase in income of many families. They leave little for the future, and when the "future" knocks, they are caught unprepared, and they find themselves in trouble.

There is a way to cope with this problem. It is to design and to carry out a "family security plan." This book will indicate how you can pursue such a plan by creating a personal investment program, obtaining adequate life insurance protection, and taking steps to preserve an estate for your family.

Other things being equal, financial security can mean the difference between a happy home and one beset by strife and worry. Statistics prove this point. A national survey showed that money problems were cited in nine out of ten cases as a major cause of divorce. Another major cause was drinking, to which people with money problems sometimes turn.

A family security plan should help you to stabilize your current financial situation as well as to build an estate that will generate future funds for the education of your children and for a comfortable life in your later years.

It should help you blunt the impact of inflation and higher taxes. The taxes and inflation have made it necessary for a family to triple its income in the last three decades just to stay even. And many families whose incomes increased faster than did taxes and inflation remained financially insecure because they failed to establish an investment program.

The idea underlying a personal investment program is quite simple. We might refer to an old-time grist mill in explaining it. The miller located his mill by a stream. He did not stop the flow of water but merely diverted some of it to turn the wheel that produced the power to grind the grain. The miller made the water work for him.

Your life's earnings might be compared to that stream of water. Year after year, the dollars flow steadily along. The object of an investment program is not to stop the flow of dollars, not to deprive your family of necessities or comforts but to divert some of those dollars so that they might work for you through investments.

Just as the miller needed a blueprint to build his mill, you will need a blueprint for your personal investment program. If your program is to succeed, it will require careful planning. This planning should start with a family budget.

Some people shrink at mention of the words "family budget." They confuse budgeting with bookkeeping. It is not. It is a blueprint for achieving a financial plan. The purpose of a budget is to help you get more from your money by cutting out inefficient spending and to guide you toward your financial goals. Besides planning, it requires determination to stick with a budget once it is formulated. To make it work, you will need the cooperation of the entire family.

A budget should be tailored to your family's needs and income. There are a number of "model" budgets which can serve as rough guidelines. But remember, a budget is a personal matter. Your goals and objectives may differ from those of your neighbors. You may place more value on education, for example, or on recreation. And geographic differences may affect the amounts allotted for such items as housing and food. One survey, for example, found that a three-bedroom house priced at $25,000 in Fort Worth, Texas, cost more than $40,000 in such areas as Chicago, Boston, and Philadelphia.

Five steps toward family security

The following five steps, adapted from a bulletin prepared by the federal government's consumer research experts, should be helpful in designing your personal budget:

Step 1. Set your goals

Before you and members of your family can work out details of a budget, you must give thought to this question: What does the family really need and want?

Priority might be assigned to those goals which benefit the family as a whole. You should try to keep your goals in line with present and estimated future income.

Your goals will fall into three categories: long-range, intermediate, and immediate. The temptation is to concentrate first on immediate goals, but it may be wiser to focus at the outset on long-term goals—those that you hope to reach in ten or twenty years or even more. Next set your intermediate goals—those for the next five years. Then list your immediate goals—those for the coming year. By using this approach, your budget will include some savings toward long-term and intermediate goals, protecting these from being sacrificed to immediate interests.

You should be as specific as possible when you set these goals. Your long-term goals might include, for example, a debt-free home, college education for your children, and savings for retirement. Your intermediate goals might cover a down payment on a house, a new car or remodeling your kitchen. Immediate goals for this year could include reducing your debts, obtaining additional life insurance, or buying a new sofa.

Remember, however, that your goals may change as the size and age of your family increase and as your income goes up or down. A newly-wed couple, for example, probably would concentrate on establishing and furnishing a home. A family with growing children likely would work toward building up a college fund. After the children are grown, parents probably will focus on completing financial arrangements for retirement years.

Once your goals are set, write them down in your budget book. This can be a looseleaf notebook or other type of fi-

How an Urban Family of Four Spends Its Money

Moderate standard of living, 1975

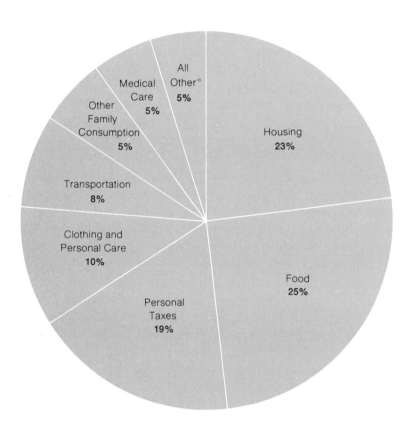

* Includes life insurance, occupational expenses, gifts, and contributions.

Source: Bureau of Labor Statistics

nancial record book available in variety and stationery stores.

Step 2. Estimate your income

Before you can plan wisely, you must know how much money you will have during the planning period. Your budget can cover any convenient period. If this is your first attempt at making a budget, you may want to set it up for a three-month period. As you gain experience, your budget can cover a twelve-month period, coinciding with the calendar year, the tax year, or the school year.

In front of your budget book, write down all funds that you expect to receive in the specified planning period. Begin with fixed amounts that both husband and wife receive regularly: wages, salaries, Social Security benefits, pension payments, and other income.

If your income is irregular or fluctuates sharply—as it may for salesmen on commission, farmers, or other self-employed persons—play it safe and make two estimates. One will be the smallest figure you can reasonably expect to receive. The other will be the largest figure. Use the low income figure as the basis for your planning. Then consider how you would use the additional amounts if you reach the higher figure.

Your estimates should also include the variable income you expect to receive in the planning period. This might include interest from savings accounts and bonds, dividends from stocks, income from rental property, and money from other sources.

One point should be stressed: Don't include in your estimates any money that you are not reasonably certain to receive. Nothing can wreck a budget faster than having a plan to spend money that you do not receive.

Step 3. Estimate your expenses

Records of past family spending can serve as a basis for

estimating current expenses. If you have not kept records, try to recall your previous expenses. Checkbook stubs, receipts, and old bills can serve as reminders.

In your budget book, list expenses that your family has been undertaking, with the amount spent on each item. Include fixed payments, such as mortgage payments and car payments, as well as contributions and other predictable expenditures.

Study the entries you have made in the various expense categories. If you are satisfied with what your dollars have given your family in the past, then allow similar amounts in your expense estimates. But if you are not satisfied with what you got for your money last month or last year, you will want to examine your spending patterns with a critical eye. Until you study your records and your budget estimates, you may be unaware of overspending and poor buying habits.

You should be realistic in revising your allowances. You may want to cut out shopping sprees and the overuse of credit, but stay flexible so that you might cope with new situations and changing conditions. For example, your family's clothing budget may go up when a child enters school, or your tax bill may climb when property valuations are updated.

It is wise to plan your large expenses so that they are spaced at intervals during the year. For example, if your daughter gets a new winter coat this month, your son might wait several months for a new suit. Or new curtains might wait until you have bought a new television set.

When you have prepared estimates of your expenses, keep them handy so that you can refer to them.

Step 4. Set up the budget

You are now ready to set up your budget, based on the three sets of calculations you already have made—your goals, your income, and your expenses.

The following form will help you in setting up your budget. You can change the form by adding or deleting categories to suit your family's needs:

Plan for Family Spending

Set asides:
 Emergency fund $_____

 Seasonal expenses   _____

 Future goals   _____

Debt payments and regular monthly expenses:
 Rent or mortgage payments $_____

 Utilities   _____

 Installment payments   _____

 Other   _____

  Total   _____

Day-to-day expenses:
 Food and beverages $_____

 Household operations,
  maintenance   _____

 Furnishings, equipment   _____

 Clothing   _____

 Personal   _____

 Transportation   _____

 Medical care   _____

 Recreation, education   _____

 Gifts, contributions   _____

 Other   _____

  Total   _____

Total set asides, debt payments, and expenses $_____

The surest way to have funds available for major expenses and future goals is to set aside money regularly—thus the "set asides" category atop the budget. The secret here is to earmark the money first, before you spend your paycheck. You may have nothing left to set aside if you wait until the end of the week or month. By setting aside a

A Guideline Budget

Compare your family's budget with that of an average family of four, given below.

	Lower Budget	Intermediate Budget	Higher Budget
Total Annual Cost	$9,588	$15,318	$22,294
Cost of Family Consumption	7,795	11,725	16,141
Food	2,952	3,827	4,819
Housing	1,857	3,533	5,353
Transportation	702	1,279	1,658
Clothing	771	1,102	1,613
Personal care	248	331	470
Medical care	818	822	857
Other family consumption *	447	831	1,371
Taxes and deductions	1,358	2,891	4,971
Social Security and disability	577	834	841
Personal income taxes	781	2,057	4,130
Other items **	436	701	1,182

* Recreation, education, and miscellaneous.
** Gifts, contributions, life insurance, and occupational expenses.

Note: Because of rounding, sums of individual items do not equal totals.

Source: Bureau of Labor Statistics

planned amount every pay period, you have greater flexibility in managing your money.

A bit of advice: It is best to keep your set-aside funds separate from your other money so you won't be tempted to spend them impulsively. You can keep them in a savings account or in government savings bonds. Thus they will be out of reach and at the same time drawing interest. The next chapter will indicate how to maximize returns on your savings.

As you start to budget, you also should allocate a fixed amount of your income to an emergency fund. Proper insurance is one of the best ways to protect your family against major financial disaster. But most families undergo minor crises not covered by insurance, which are too large to be absorbed by a day-to-day budget. An example might be the collapse of a washing machine or an unexpected series of medical bills.

Once you decide how large a cushion you need for meeting emergencies, you can then work out the amount to be set aside each month or week. Bear in mind that your emergency fund is a safeguard, not an investment. Keep it in a savings account or other form that will enable you to get it quickly when you need it.

Now you can proceed to a second category of set-asides —seasonal expenses. As every family knows, some large expenses occur seasonally, such as taxes on real estate, personal property, and income; school books and supplies; life insurance; fuel and travel. Other expenses in this category might include car license plates, medical checkups, Christmas gifts, season tickets to baseball or football games, or tickets to a concert series.

These expenses generally can be anticipated and included in your budget for the year. If you set aside a definite amount each month, spreading the cost over a twelve-month period, you can more easily meet such bills when they fall due. If your personal property tax is $600 a year, for example, you can reach this amount by setting aside $50 a month for a year.

Now we come to the third, and perhaps most important, category of set-asides: future goals.

For your immediate and intermediate goals, assign a dollar value to each and set a date you hope to achieve these amounts. Then translate the dollar figure into the amount that must be saved each budget period. This money, of course, can go into savings accounts that will pay interest and thereby help you reach these goals faster.

You should also set dollar costs and dates for your long-range goals, but you might consider a different approach this time. Rather than simply piling up money in a bank account, you might want to use this money for other investments. A wide range of investment opportunities are available that might sprout and produce more money for better meeting long-range goals or sustaining the family in future years. We will examine such opportunities in succeeding chapters.

Now that you have completed the set-aside category, you can proceed to list the other expenses you expect to have during each budget period. You can estimate quite accurately your family's regular—or fixed—expenses. These may include rent or mortgage payments, hospital and health insurance premiums, bills for electricity, gas, water, telephone, school tuition, and other regular expenses.

When you have listed your regular expenses, you are ready to calculate your day-to-day expenses, those that vary from week to week or month to month. These are the most flexible entries in your budget, and thus are the easiest to cut when you need to economize.

Your records will help you estimate how much you have been spending on food, clothing, transportation, and other budget items. Then you will have to decide whether you want to keep spending approximately the same amounts, or whether you want to make some adjustments. Many of your smaller immediate goals may fit better under the various day-to-day categories than under the set-aside category. For example, a new wardrobe for a college-bound daughter can go under clothing. A kitchen stool and room-size rug can go under furnishings and equipment. In addition, it usually is a good idea to give each member of the family a small allowance that need not be accounted for.

Step 5. Balance expenses and income

Now for the moment of truth: Add up the figures in your spending plan and compare the total with your estimate of income for the planning period.

If the two figures are roughly in balance, you are in good form. If your income exceeds your estimate of expenses, you have the luxury of deciding whether to satisfy immediate desires or to increase the amount being set aside for future goals, including those you hope to reach through an investment program.

If your expenses exceed your income, as frequently happens, you must re-evaluate your spending plan with an eye to cutting expenses. Ask yourself: Can I postpone or drop some items?

It may be wise to make budget cutting a family project, with each member suggesting economies he or she is willing to accept. Many kinds of adjustments can be made. For example, mother may decide to make clothing for the children in order to save money for music lessons. Or father may settle for a smaller, less expensive car so as to be able to meet the cost of the vacation the family would like to have.

Examine your regular expenses with a critical eye. You may need to reduce or eliminate installment payments and other fixed obligations. Perhaps your family should consider converting endowment to a cheaper form of insurance, or trading in your large car for a smaller one that costs less to operate.

If, after cutting expenses, you still are unable to balance your budget, you may need to consider ways of increasing your family's income. This subject will be explored later in this chapter.

Putting your budget to work

Once you take these five steps, you will have put your spending plan on paper. You will then want to try it out. To carry out your budget, you will need to develop good buying habits. You will also need to keep records. They will tell you if your dollars are giving your family what it really needs and wants. Make your records simple. You don't need a detailed account of where you spend every penny. But you do need to know where your money goes.

One way to get spending reports from members of the

family is to have them put receipts on a spindle each day. Or each member of the family can slip a note into the record book for the family "bookkeeper." At the end of the week, add up amounts spent and enter them in your financial record book. Then, at the end of the month, total the expenditures under each category and compare them with those in your plan. It is a good idea to keep all financial records together. You may find it helpful to set aside a desk drawer, a box, or some other convenient place to put your record book and bills, receipts, and other financial papers such as paycheck stubs.

If your records disclose that your spending is deviating from your plan, find out why. By asking the question "why" and finding the answers, you should be able to improve your spending plan.

If you follow the plan and discover that it does not provide for your family's needs, you will have to revise it. On the other hand, if the plan suits your needs but you fail to stick to it, you obviously will have to make greater efforts at self-discipline and better management.

Remember this: A budget is something to be worked and reworked until it "fits" your family and satisfies individual members. Don't expect to find a perfect budget the first time you set one up. But with each succeeding budget you can expect improvement.

And even when you come up with a satisfactory spending plan, don't be surprised if you need to change it from time to time. As your family situation changes, you will need to reorganize your budget around new goals, needs, and wants.

Boosting your income

As noted earlier, some families find that they are unable to balance their budget with their current income. They then seek additional revenue, which might come from a wife who takes a job, from a husband who starts "moon-

How Taxes Affect Incomes of Working Wives In Different Economic Groups

Level of husband's taxable income* excluding wife's salary	Wife's Gross Salary					
	$2,000	$4,000	$6,000	$8,000	$10,000	$12,000
	Wife's Take-home Pay after Taxes					
$ 8,000	1,343	2,686	3,969	5,252	6,475	7,698
12,000	1,283	2,566	3,789	5,012	6,155	7,298
16,000	1,223	2,446	3,589	4,732	5,795	6,858
20,000	1,143	2,286	3,349	4,412	5,415	6,418
24,000	1,063	2,126	3,129	4,132	5,075	6,018
32,000	943	1,886	2,769	3,652	4,475	5,298

* Includes 5 percent state tax (may vary from state to state), 5.85 percent Social Security tax, and federal income tax.

In most states, it is cheaper taxwise to file separate state returns in the case of a working wife. Families in which both parents work are eligible for an income tax credit for child-care expenses.

lighting," or from some kind of business at home.

According to estimates, over fifteen million married women have jobs outside the home. Several factors should be considered before a wife and mother considers taking a job. Going to work costs money. There are direct and indirect costs which must be weighed against the financial benefits. Experts say you should consider such questions as these: Will you need someone to clean house and care for the children? Is your present wardrobe adequate, or will you need more clothes? What will your transportation costs be? How much of your earnings will go to pay additional income tax?

This last question can be a major one. The wife's income, when added to the husband's, can place the family in a higher tax bracket. If, for example, the husband's taxable income is $12,000 before his wife takes a job, and her gross salary is $4,000, she will have a take-home pay after taxes of less than $2,600. If her gross salary is $8,000, and her husband's taxable income is $12,000, her take-home pay after taxes would barely exceed $5,000. At higher levels of income, taxes are proportionately higher, and the net earnings of working couples suffer accordingly.

In some cases, a wife can realize nearly as much net income working part-time as she would working full-time. She can, for example, cut down on her baby-sitter costs, especially if the children are in school part of the day. The situation varies from family to family, but according to one rough guideline, a mother working part-time may keep 70 cents of each dollar she earns, while a mother working full-time may keep only 50 cents.

This can be seen in the case of a woman earning $100 a week as a full-time secretary. Her expenses, including taxes, transportation, lunches, child care, clothing and extra household costs, totaled $51 a week, leaving her $49. When she took a part-time job at $50 a week, she was able to eliminate the need of a baby-sitter and she was able to eat lunches at home. Her expenses, including taxes, transportation, clothing and extra household costs, came to less than $15 a week, leaving a net of $35.

An estimated three million American men hold part-time "moonlighting" jobs, working on the average between ten and fifteen hours a week. Many are between the ages of twenty-five and forty-five, the period when family expenses usually are highest. The second jobs often are temporary, taken to ease the burden of unexpected medical bills, to build up a savings account for a down payment on a house, or to start an investment program.

There are some disadvantages to moonlighting. The first, of course, is possible damage to health. By taking on too big a load, you may find yourself running down physically. You may find, too, that you will not be able to spend enough time with your family. There are also extra expenses to be considered. For example, a father taking a second job on weekends may have to hire someone to mow the lawn. He may have to buy special clothes or equipment, and he may have the extra expense of eating in a restaurant. Such additional costs can erode extra income and naturally must be taken into account when moonlighting is being considered.

With your goals in mind and with a program for achieving them outlined in your budget, you might next consider the various opportunities indicated in subsequent chapters for investing your savings and your capital.

CHAPTER 2

First
Steps
Toward
Security

American families are caught in a two-way squeeze. Inflation erodes the purchasing power of their dollars. And as they work harder to increase their income to meet rising prices, they automatically move into a higher tax bracket, and taxes then take a bigger bite out of their paychecks.

The squeeze can be illustrated graphically in the case of John and Jane Smith—an "average" American couple with two children. Suppose their gross income in 1950 was $10,000. After taxes, they would have had spendable income of about $8,800. But twenty-five years later, to have the same spendable income in "real" dollars, their gross income would have had to be roughly $20,000. Inflation and higher taxes would have taken the rest of their income.

Further statistical proof of the squeeze came in the mid-1970s when the government reported that while median family income was increasing at a rate of more than 6 percent a year, inflation was increasing even faster—meaning that "real" income was going down instead of up.

In recent years, the government has set guidelines and attempted other methods to check the rate of inflation, but it still has continued at a rate of 5 percent or more.

A dollar worth 100 cents today would be worth only 75 cents five years from now at a 5 percent rate of inflation. In ten years, it would be worth about 56 cents. In fifteen years, it would be worth less than half the present value.

Looking at it another way, if you needed $1,000 a month to retire today and your cost of living was rising by 5 percent a year, in five years you would need $1,276 a month. In ten years you would need $1,629. In twenty years, you would need $2,653.

The impact of rising costs will be felt especially by those sending children to college. Projections based on government figures, assuming a 3 percent annual rise in the cost of living, indicate that average annual costs of a college education will nearly double between 1970 and 1980. A publicly-supported college that charged $1,273 for tuition, fees, room and board in 1970 will be asking $1,950 in 1980, according to these projections. A private college charging $2,712 for these items in 1970 will be demanding $4,545 in 1980.

These figures underscore the importance of developing a family security plan and of starting now on a personal investment program. A budget can help you to get the most for your current spending. And a personal investment program can help you reach such long-term goals as a retirement or college education fund by overcoming the inflation-taxation squeeze.

The sooner you begin, the less painful it will be. Suppose, for example, that you want to accumulate $50,000 by the time you reach retirement age of sixty-five. If you begin at age thirty-five, you will need to set aside $60.64 monthly in fixed dollar savings earning 5 percent interest compounded

The Rising Cost of a Year in College

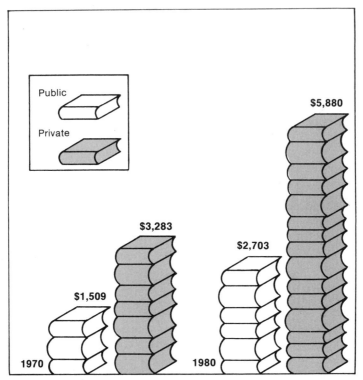

Public
Private

$5,880

$3,283

$2,703

$1,509

1970

1980

Source: Vance, Sanders & Co.

semiannually to reach that goal. If you start when you are forty-five, you must set aside $122.36 monthly—more than twice the amount had you started at age thirty-five. And if you start at age fifty-five, you must set aside $322.86 monthly—more than five times the amount had you started at age thirty-five.

These figures should make clear that the sooner you begin a serious savings and investment program, the easier it will be to reach your long-range goals.

Monthly Amount Needed for Retirement

Annual Rate of Inflation	Today	In 5 Years	In 10 Years	In 20 Years	In 30 Years
3%	$1,000	$1,159	$1,344	$1,806	$2,427
4%	$1,000	$1,217	$1,480	$2,191	$3,243
5%	$1,000	$1,276	$1,629	$2,653	$4,322
6%	$1,000	$1,338	$1,791	$3,207	$5,743

Source: Vance, Sanders & Co.

Where to put your savings

Investment opportunities are varied. They include real estate, common and preferred stocks, corporate, government and municipal bonds, mutual funds and annuities.

But before you can make any of these investments, you must have money. Unless you are lucky enough to find or to inherit a fortune, you must save to get that money.

You are saving money when you make a payment on your home mortgage, since you are buying property that can be turned into cash. The same is true of many life insurance policies, since they contain cash value features. But in a narrow sense, saving means the accumulation of a cash fund that can be invested or held.

For employees, one of the least painful methods of saving is through the payroll deduction plan. The employer withholds from each paycheck a specified sum, which is placed in a savings account or is used to purchase United States savings bonds. Since the employee never sees or touches the money, he doesn't have to fight the temptation to spend it instead of putting it aside. Even small amounts saved regularly can grow into impressive sums.

As your savings begin to grow, you might keep this rule in mind: Don't use money for investments that you may need for something else. In other words, maintain an easily accessible emergency fund.

Even the most carefully planned and executed investment program may take years to accomplish. In the meantime, as the economy fluctuates, the value of your investment may drop below the price you paid for it. If for some reason you need money badly and have no reserve fund, you may have to sell your investment at a substantial loss. But if you have an emergency fund, you can take the ups and downs of investing in stride, free from pressure and worry.

How big should this emergency fund be?

According to one rule of thumb, a family should be able to live for six months without its usual source of income. Some authorities say a fund equivalent to three months' take-home pay may be adequate for emergencies.

This emergency fund can be earning interest or dividends and growing in value while giving you peace of mind. You may be surprised to discover how short a time it takes to *double* your money simply by letting it draw compound interest. A $1,000 savings account that pays 6 percent interest compounded annually will grow to $2,000 in twelve years. This is possible because the interest earned is added to your account and in turn starts drawing interest itself.

The accompanying chart shows how long it takes to double your money at different rates of interest, compounded annually.

One of the most dramatic illustrations of the way money will multiply itself with compound interest is found in the case of a $5,000 gift Benjamin Franklin gave the residents of Boston in 1791.

When he bequeathed the sum, Franklin attached the proviso that it be allowed to accumulate compound interest

Doubling Your Money

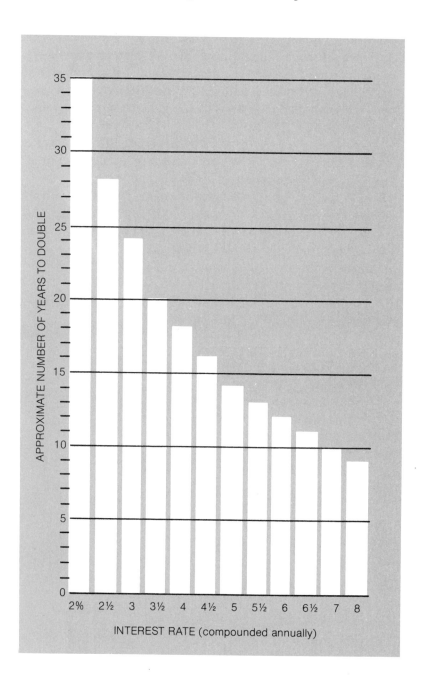

for 200 years. One hundred years later, in 1891, the fund had grown to $322,000. Part of the money then was used to construct a school building, and the rest was set aside for a second hundred years of accumulation. By 1961, with thirty years yet to go before the end of the second century, the fund exceeded $17 million! The original $5,000 had multiplied itself 3,400 times.

Your emergency fund can be kept in one or several places. Let's look at the major factors to be considered in selecting a place for your savings.

The ideal savings institution, of course, would be a convenient one offering maximum safety while paying the highest return on readily liquid funds. Consider yourself lucky if you find such a place, because the perfect repository is rare. One possible compromise: divide your money among two or more choices.

Here, in capsule form, is how financial experts rate the places where you can put your savings:

• *Commercial bank:* Safe, liquid, convenient, but sometimes a lower rate of interest than available elsewhere.

• *Savings bank:* Safe, liquid, medium rate of interest, but not locally available in some parts of the country.

• *Savings and loan association:* Safe, convenient, good rate of dividend, but does not offer the convenience of a checking account.

• *Credit union:* Convenient, liquid, medium rate of interest. Credit unions have acquired the federal deposit insurance available at most other savings institutions.

• *U.S. savings bonds:* Safe, liquid, convenient, but pay a low interest rate in early years after purchase.

Now let's examine in more detail the advantages and disadvantages of these savings institutions.

Commercial banks

Commercial banks have been called "department stores

of finance" because they perform so many financial functions. They offer checking and savings accounts. They make business, personal, mortgage, and other types of loans. They rent safe deposit boxes, give investment advice, perform trust services, sell traveler's checks, and even handle payment of utility bills for their customers.

Because of the variety of services it offers, a commercial bank can be a convenient place to keep your savings. Besides the traditional passbook savings account, many banks offer savings certificates and other time deposit plans at relatively high interest rates. Some years ago, many banks were paying low interest, often 2 percent, on savings. But recently a number of commercial banks have aggressively sought savings accounts by offering interest rates of 5 percent on passbook accounts and higher rates on certificates of deposit.

At one time, commercial banks paid interest on checking accounts too. But because of runs on banks during the Great Depression, the government now prohibits any bank it controls from paying interest on "demand deposits,"— deposits in a checking account which can be withdrawn without notice. Banks paying interest may require a depositor to give written notice, usually thirty days, before he withdraws his savings. In practice, this notice is not required, and savings can be withdrawn at any time.

Banks vary in the way they compute interest on savings accounts. One survey found more than 100 different methods in use by commercial banks. Traditionally banks have credited interest to savings accounts semi-annually. The trend now is toward crediting it on a quarterly basis. Some banks using computers to help with the calculations advertise "daily interest," paying interest from the day the money is deposited. Usually interest commences on the first day of the month following a deposit. In some cases, deposits made by the tenth of the month receive interest from the first day of the month.

It pays to pick the bank which uses the most favorable method of calculation. Compounding of interest makes a difference. When 4 percent interest is compounded semi-annually, the actual yield is 4.04 percent. When it is compounded quarterly, the yield is 4.06 percent.

Some banks pay interest only on the lowest balance for the quarterly or semi-annual interest period. Thus, if you began the interest period with $1,000 on deposit, withdrew all but $100, then later built the account back up to $1,000, the bank would pay you interest only on the $100. A bank offering "daily interest" would pay you interest for the time the $1,000 was in the bank.

Deposits in all but a handful of the nation's commercial banks are insured up to a maximum of $40,000 by the government-sponsored Federal Deposit Insurance Corporation (FDIC). If an insured bank fails, the agency either pays the depositor directly for his loss or opens an account in the same amount for him at a nearby bank. The $40,000 protection limit applies to a single depositor in a given bank, no matter how many accounts he may have. For example, if you had a $2,000 balance in your checking account and a $39,000 savings account in the same bank, you would receive $40,000—not $41,000—if the bank failed. But the law does not prevent the depositor from spreading his funds among several banks or among several accounts in family names at the same bank. For example, if you were fortunate enough to have $120,000, you could keep it in insured accounts in the same bank by holding one $40,000 account in your name, another $40,000 account in your wife's or husband's name, and a third $40,000 in a joint account with your wife or husband "with the right of survivorship." In such a joint account, if one depositor dies the surviving co-owner gets the whole sum.

Commercial banks will pay interest on your savings deposits, but profits go to their stockholders.

Savings banks

Mutual savings banks offer many of the services of commercial banks. The major difference is that, in theory, profits go to the benefit of depositors, who are the shareholders.

The first savings banks were formed in 1816 in Boston and Philadelphia. Now there are about 500 savings banks in the eighteen states that charter them—Alaska, Connecticut, Delaware, Indiana, Maine, Maryland, Massachusetts, Minnesota, New Hampshire, New Jersey, New York, Ohio, Oregon, Pennsylvania, Rhode Island, Vermont, Washington, and Wisconsin. Some savings banks have grown into huge financial institutions. More than ten banks have deposits of $100 million and more.

Deposits in all savings banks total about $115 billion. These deposits generally are placed in sound investments, such as home mortgages, U.S. Government bonds, and high-grade securities.

Most mutual savings banks pay 5 percent or more interest on deposits. This interest—technically dividends—is entered in the passbook you receive when you open an account. In most savings banks, the passbook must be presented when making a deposit or withdrawal.

Care should be taken not to lose your passbook. If you do happen to lose it, you may have to pay the expense of advertising its loss in a newspaper before another passbook would be issued to you.

Almost all savings banks carry some type of deposit insurance. About 350 are members of the Federal Deposit Insurance Corporation, and their depositors have the same protection against loss as do depositors in member commercial banks. Several states offer savings banks a form of deposit insurance similar to FDIC.

A majority of the nation's savings banks do not impose a service charge on accounts. While savings banks do not have checking accounts, they provide many of the same services as commercial banks—passbook, loans, banking by mail, safe deposit boxes, sale of money orders and traveler's checks, and special accounts for Christmas or vacation savings.

Savings and loan associations

Savings and loan associations perform a two-fold service. They are among the most popular savings institutions in the United States. They also are a major source for home mortgages.

About one-third of the dollars saved by individuals in the nation are deposited in savings and loan associations. A reason for their popularity is that they generally pay a slightly higher interest rate on savings than do commercial banks. When banks are paying 5 percent interest, most savings and loan associations usually are paying $5\frac{1}{4}$ percent or more. The higher interest rate is possible because of the high yield on mortgage loans. These associations place most of their assets—up to 95 percent—on loan in mortgages.

The nation's first savings and loan association was established in a suburb of Philadelphia in 1831. Thirty-seven members pooled their savings. When money accumulated, the first loan to build a house was made. Other members postponed their home building plans until more money accumulated. Soon it became apparent that more savings accounts were needed to supply a steady flow of funds for home financing. Today fifty-five million people save in the more than 5,200 savings and loan associations in the United States. These savings have been invested in about sixteen million mortgages.

Some of the present associations are known as building and loan associations. In New England, they are called co-operative banks; in Louisiana, homestead associations. About one-third of all savings and loan associations are federally chartered. The rest are state licensed.

Nine out of ten savings and loan associations are mutual corporations. This means they are owned by their depositors. A depositor in the association technically is buying shares on which he receives dividends (interest). Legally he is a shareholder. In contrast, the depositor in a commercial bank is a creditor of the bank, which owes him the money he has placed in it.

Many different types of accounts with a variety of names have been developed by savings and loan institutions. The two most common types are:

• *Savings Accounts:* This, the most popular type, may be opened with any amount of money. Deposits and withdrawals may be made in any amount and are recorded in the customer's passbook. Dividends are credited to the account either quarterly or semi-annually.

• *Investment Certificates:* Investment savings accounts and investment savings certificates usually pay a higher rate of interest than passbook savings accounts. They require a larger deposit than a passbook savings account, and the money is not so readily available.

The investor buys certificates in units of $100, $300, $500 or more. Savings institutions offer a variety of plans. Banks as well as savings and loan associations have been promoting investment certificates. Some mail dividend checks periodically. Others require the investor to leave his money on deposit for a specified period—three months, one year, or longer. Principal plus interest is returned at the end of this period. The certificates pay as much as 1 percent more than passbook savings accounts. The maximum interest ranges from 6 percent to 7¾ percent.

Savings and loan associations do not offer checking accounts. But they do offer other services almost identical to those of banks—Christmas savings accounts, safe deposit boxes, money orders, and general investment and financial advice.

Savings and loan associations may require a thirty- to ninety-day written notice of withdrawal, but normally they pay out savings on demand. The requirement for written

How Your Savings Can Grow

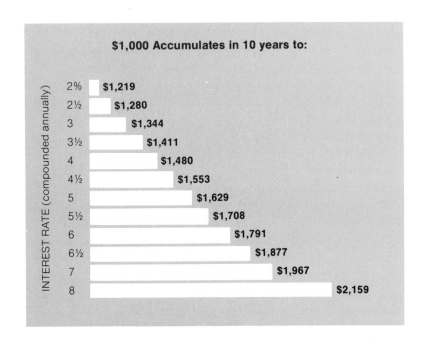

$1,000 Accumulates in 10 years to:

INTEREST RATE (compounded annually)

2%	$1,219
2½	$1,280
3	$1,344
3½	$1,411
4	$1,480
4½	$1,553
5	$1,629
5½	$1,708
6	$1,791
6½	$1,877
7	$1,967
8	$2,159

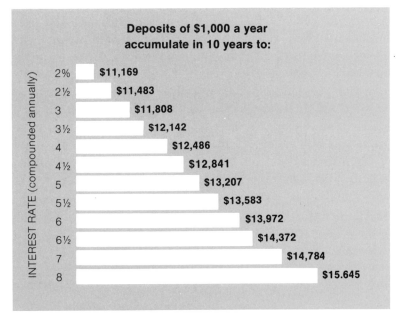

Deposits of $1,000 a year accumulate in 10 years to:

INTEREST RATE (compounded annually)

2%	$11,169
2½	$11,483
3	$11,808
3½	$12,142
4	$12,486
4½	$12,841
5	$13,207
5½	$13,583
6	$13,972
6½	$14,372
7	$14,784
8	$15.645

notice is designed for use only in periods of financial crisis, such as a severe depression.

Most of the larger associations belong to the Federal Savings and Loan Insurance Corporation, which insures savings accounts up to a maximum of $40,000 each. This is similar to the FDIC insurance held by commercial banks. If an insured savings and loan association fails, its shareholders get new accounts in another association not in default. Because of close state and federal regulation, and continuing prosperity, the number of savings and loan associations that have failed in recent years has been small.

Credit unions

A credit union is an association of individuals who agree to pool their savings and make the money available as loans to members. The members of the credit union have a common interest. They may be employees of the same company or members of a fraternal order or labor union. They obtain a state or federal charter when they form the credit union. Members elect officers and set policies at annual meetings.

Credit unions are not new. The credit union movement in the United States can be traced to the turn of the century. Massachusetts passed the first state credit union law in 1909, and since then most states have followed suit. In 1934, Congress passed a law providing federal charters for credit unions. Today the nation's 25,000 credit unions have more than twenty-seven million members and total assets of more than $28 billion.

Credit unions generally offer attractive interest rates on both savings and loans. A recent national survey showed that more than 75 percent of the federally chartered credit unions paid 5 percent or more interest on savings. Some were paying 6 percent interest.

Credit unions can pay handsome interest on savings because they are non-profit associations and have limited

overhead. Officers and directors often serve without pay.
Sponsoring organizations or employers frequently donate
office space. And credit unions are tax-exempt.

To join a credit union, a member buys at least one share,
usually for $5. Technically, savings by members are in the
form of share purchases, but in practice most credit unions
accept savings as small as 25 cents a week. Credit unions
encourage members to save regularly, promoting the habit
of systematic thrift. A payroll deduction plan is often used
for the purchase of shares.

In most credit unions, $5,000 is the maximum savings ac-
count allowed. Average savings are about $650, a national
survey shows. Although the credit union may require advance notice for withdrawal of savings, this provision is
seldom invoked.

Some credit unions provide life insurance to depositors.
Some match each savings dollar with a dollar of insurance
on the life of the depositor, free of extra charge.

Credit unions are not allowed to charge their members
more than 1 percent interest per month on the unpaid balance of a loan. This comes to an annual true interest rate
of 12 percent. Some credit unions charge three-fourths of 1
percent interest per month. This equals an annual true interest of 9 percent. It may sound high, but it compares fa-
vorably with the advance-discount loans offered by many
banks. A borrower obtaining an advance-discount loan pays
the interest on the total sum first, then pays off the principal month by month. A 6 percent advance-discount loan is
the equivalent of a true interest rate of 12 percent. Credit
unions have suffered surprisingly few losses on their loans
—about two-tenths of 1 percent of all loans made.

The most effective credit unions offer financial counseling
to members. Low-income, debt-ridden families have been
nursed back to financial health by their credit unions. In
addition to advice, credit unions have made loans enabling
families to pay their debts and repay the money borrowed

in weekly installments they can manage without hardship.

Most credit unions do not have the professional management of banks and other savings institutions. However, they have federal insurance protecting deposits up to $40,000, and they are required to set aside a reserve against losses. Their records are audited regularly, and their officers are bonded.

Savings bonds

United States savings bonds are among the most popular methods of saving money. And they are among the safest, since the credit of the United States Government stands behind them. The two most commonly purchased types of U.S. savings bonds are:

• *Series E*—These are bought at a 25 percent discount and increase in value to their full face amount in five years.

• *Series H*—These are "current income" bonds. The buyers pay the full face amount and receive interest payments by check twice a year.

Of the two, Series E bonds are the more widely bought. They can be purchased in denominations as small as $25 and as large as $1,000. Payroll deduction plans for purchasing the bonds are available through many employers. And most commercial banks offer "bond-a-month" plans. The bank deducts the cost of the bond from the individual's checking account at regular intervals and purchases the bond for him. Savings bonds also can be purchased at other financial institutions.

From time to time, the government has increased the yield on Series E bonds by reducing the amount of time it takes for them to mature. During and after World War II, when numerous drives were conducted to spur the sale of savings bonds, it took ten years for a bond to grow from 75 percent of face value to full face value. This provided an average annual yield of 2.9 percent if held to maturity. Now, Series E bonds mature in five years, providing an average annual yield of 6 percent compounded semi-annually if held to maturity.

This yield is about the same as interest rates on savings accounts at many banks and savings and loan associations. But the commercial interest rate generally is not guaranteed for as long a period. Interest received on savings accounts must be reported as taxable income in the year during which it is credited to the account, while interest on Series E bonds is not taxable until the bond is cashed in, unless the bond owner wishes to pay taxes currently on the interest.

Series H bonds can be bought in denominations of $500, $1,000 and $5,000. The investor pays the full face amount when he purchases the bond, and he gets the full face amount back when he cashes it in. A check for the interest is mailed to the investor twice a year. If held to maturity, Series H bonds earn an average annual return of 6 percent. Income taxes must be paid on the interest in the year received.

Both Series E and Series H bonds can be purchased in the name of one person, in the names of two persons as co-owners, or in the name of one person payable on death to another designated person.

For example, when John Smith buys a bond he can have it registered in one of these three ways:

(1) John H. Smith
123 Main Street, Anytown, U.S.A.

(2) John H. Smith
123 Main Street, Anytown, U.S.A. or Mrs. Mary E. Smith

(3) John H. Smith
123 Main Street, Anytown, U.S.A.
Payable on death to Mrs. Mary E. Smith

Under the co-ownership option, either owner can cash in the bond without the consent of the other. If one of the owners dies, the other becomes sole owner without having to establish proof of death or transferring the bond to his name.

If a bond owner wants to change co-ownership or change the beneficiary he would have to cash in the bond and buy a new one.

You may be able to shift income to a lower tax bracket, and thus save on taxes, if you buy savings bonds in your child's name. In that case, you ought to file a tax return for your child next year and report the annual interest. After the first time that savings bond interest is declared on a child's return, he or she does not have to fill out another return until total income is large enough to require a return to be filed. It is assumed for tax purposes that the interest is being declared annually.

The Treasury Department records each bond by its number and the name of the owner, and will replace bonds which are lost, stolen, or destroyed. In such a case, the bond owner should write the Bureau of Public Debt, Post Office Box 509, Parkersburg, West Virginia 26101.

Faster replacement is made if the owner reports the bond's serial number and date of purchase. A list of such numbers and dates should be recorded by the owner and kept separate from his bonds to be available in the event of loss.

Summing up:

• When you have saved from three to six months' earnings and deposited them where you can reach them readily, you have achieved your emergency fund. Indeed, you are well on the way to a personal investment program and a planned estate to leave to your family.

• A savings program is a prerequisite to any investment plan. Planning should start with a family budget. Remember, budgeting isn't bookkeeping. Budgeting is intended to help you look ahead, not keep track of the past.

• You will find it easier to save if you keep in mind that you are purchasing something substantial, a basic necessity of modern life, future security for you and your family.

• It is important to keep part of your savings where the money will be available when you need it. You can open accounts in one or several savings institutions—in a commercial bank, a savings bank, a savings and loan association, a credit union. You can purchase United States savings bonds. Consider the advantages and disadvantages of each before making a decision.

Once you have obtained your short-term goal, you are ready to consider a long-range investment program. The money you invest for long-range goals is not needed immediately. Therefore you can consider a wide variety of investments, many of them offering a far higher return than does a saving institution. They include home ownership, commercial real estate, stocks and bonds. We next examine the advantages and disadvantages of each.

CHAPTER 3

Where to Invest Your Money

The magic in building an estate which will go on producing income after a breadwinner himself has ceased to be productive is to be found in the powerful force called "investment." It is the investment of money in productive activity which can produce rewards in relative abundance. The great challenge to all Americans—one which can make the difference between a secure and an insecure life—is to find those investments which will generate a sufficient supply of funds to meet one's needs and desires.

Opportunities for investment in the United States are countless, and one must have an overall view of their scope so as to be able to choose. You can invest in a home, a cooperative apartment, a condominium, in land and buildings, in common stock, preferred stock, corporate bonds, federal, state and municipal bonds, to mention some of the major categories.

Drawing up a family balance sheet

Before examining the different areas of investment, it might be wise to consider drawing up a family balance sheet. Corporations use a balance sheet to show where they stand. You can use it for the same purpose. It will give you a figure for your net worth—or net indebtedness—and thereby indicate the overall state of your financial situation. It will help you decide whether your net worth is growing fast enough and whether changes in investments already made should seriously be considered. In event of net indebtedness, such a balance sheet may help spur you to take corrective action.

If you review your balance sheet at least once a year, you will be putting your overall personal economic affairs on a serious, businesslike basis.

You can draw up a balance sheet in a matter of minutes. You might start by drawing a line down the middle of a sheet of paper. On one side, list all your assets—the things you own—and their value. On the other side, list all liabilities—what you owe and the amounts. The difference between the two totals is your net worth or, if liabilities are greater than assets, your net indebtedness.

On the assets side of the sheet, the list might include:

—Home furnishings, such as furniture and appliances; tools in your workshop and outdoor equipment.

—Cash on hand and in checking and savings accounts.

—Automobiles at market or trade-in value.

—House and other real estate at market value.

—Personal property, such as clothing, jewelry, cameras, a boat, and sports equipment.

—The cash value of life insurance policies, pension plans, and annuity contracts.

—Stocks and corporate and government bonds at current market value.

—Money loaned to others.

On the liabilities side of the sheet, the list might include:

—Unpaid mortgage on house and other real estate.

—Balance of your automobile loan.

—Bills due on charge accounts, installment purchases, and medical expenses.

—Money you have borrowed. Loans from relatives, banks, or against the cash value of a life insurance policy.

Having drawn up your balance sheet, you might go on to consider the opportunities and alternatives for investment.

Buying a home

About six out of every ten American families own their own homes. The purchase of a home is the largest single investment many ever make. Careful planning is needed to determine the place of home ownership in your investment program.

Most people assume you save money in the long run if you buy a home rather than rent a house or an apartment. This may be true in some sections of the country, especially where apartments and other rental housing are scarce. But in other areas, where land and building costs are high, a family might discover that it is cheaper to rent than to buy.

There are psychological factors to keep in mind. Some families thrive on apartment and urban living. Others find that home ownership gives them a sense of security and belonging.

A home with the mortgage reduced or paid off can be an important asset since real estate tends to gain in value over the years, particularly in an inflationary economy.

How much should you pay for a home?

In years past, the rule was that you should not buy a home with a price tag more than twice your annual income. Today it is considered acceptable to buy a home costing as much as three times your annual income. Using this rule of thumb, a person with a $15,000 annual income is in a position to look at homes in the $40,000 to $45,000 price range. A person with a $25,000 annual income can consider homes in the $65,000 to $75,000 range.

Other factors can modify this general rule. The main ones are the size of the down payment, the number of persons in the family, other financial obligations, and the certainty of the annual income.

Under the government's mortgage insurance programs, many families are able to buy homes with a small down payment or, in some cases, no down payment at all. But many financial counselors recommend that a family make a down payment equal at least to 10 percent of the total purchase price of their home. Others suggest a 20 percent down payment. These authorities point out that the larger initial investment reduces the size of the mortgage and thus cuts down the amount of the monthly interest and principal payments.

In the long run, it is cheaper to keep the mortgage repayment period as short as possible. Let's assume you plan to buy a home costing $30,000. If you make a down payment of $5,000 and pay all closing costs, the mortgage would amount to $25,000. This table illustrates how the length of the repayment period can affect the monthly, annual, and total cost of that $25,000 mortgage (assuming 8 percent interest):

Payment	20-year Mortgage	25-year Mortgage	30-year Mortgage
Monthly	$ 209.00	$ 193.00	$ 183.50
Yearly	$ 2,511.00	$ 2,316.00	$ 2,202.00
Total	$50,220.00	$57,900.00	$66,060.00

If you select the 25-year repayment period instead of the 20-year period, your monthly payments will be $16 a month

More and More People
Are Buying Homes

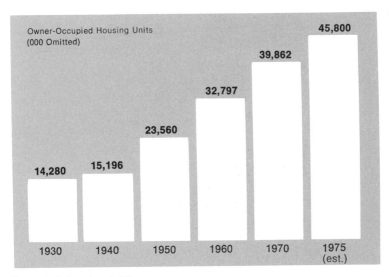

Owner-Occupied Housing Units
(000 Omitted)

Year	Value
1930	14,280
1940	15,196
1950	23,560
1960	32,797
1970	39,862
1975 (est.)	45,800

Source: U.S. Department of Commerce

less. But you end up paying $7,680 more in interest charges. Monthly payments on the 30-year mortgage are $25.50 a month lower, but the total cost is $15,840 higher than for the 20-year mortgage.

The figures shown in the table do not include taxes, insurance, utilities, or maintenance costs. These expenses should be taken into account when you consider buying a home. As a general rule, allow about one-half of 1 percent of the purchase price per year for maintenance and about one-third of 1 percent per year for insurance. For a $50,000 home, this would mean budgeting about $250 a year for maintenance costs and about $167 a year for insurance.

It is more difficult to generalize about the costs of taxes and utilities. These costs vary widely, depending upon a particular community's tax rate and upon the climate in different parts of the country. A potential home owner can make inquiries of city or county officials to determine what the annual taxes would be. Acquaintances who are home owners can help you estimate the cost of utilities.

There could be additional expenses associated with home ownership. New homes may require landscaping. Older homes may need repairs or alterations.

A family may face a decision on whether to buy an existing home or build a new one. A new home may cost you more than you expect. Many families tend to improve upon building plans as the structure takes shape. Unless there is some extra money tucked away to cover these changes, it is best to stick closely to the original blueprints. If you are thinking seriously about buying an existing home, consider hiring a professional appraiser to inspect the house and make certain it is structurally sound. Fees usually range upward from $50. This could save you a lot of money in repairs and maintenance costs.

There are certain tax advantages to home ownership. Interest charges on a home mortgage are deductible in figuring federal income taxes. So are property taxes. But remember that these tax regulations could be changed in the future.

Buying your own apartment

More and more apartment dwellers are buying their own apartments or a share in the apartment buildings where they live. As proprietors, they gain the same tax advantages as home owners, acquire some say in the operation of the building, and frequently make sizeable profits on their investments.

Cooperatives and condominiums are the two types of apartment ownership available. The condominium owner actually owns his own apartment. The tenant who buys into a cooperative buys a share in the corporation which owns the building.

The person purchasing a cooperative apartment receives

shares in the corporation and a proprietary (proprietor's) lease. He gets a vote in the operation of the corporation, but he also agrees to abide by its rules. Tenants share the costs of operation, maintenance, repairs, taxes, mortgage, insurance, and other expenses for the whole building. In addition, each tenant decorates and maintains his own apartment. As stockholders, the tenants elect the board of directors of the cooperative.

Annual expenses vary widely, but a cooperative apartment usually costs less than a comparable rented apartment. Some well-established cooperatives are non-profit organizations owned outright by the tenants. Some cooperatives are heavily mortgaged real estate promotions. The promoter makes his profit on the initial sale of shares. The tenant builds his equity—his interest in the corporation—as the mortgage is paid off.

There are some disadvantages to cooperative ownership. Maintenance and repair charges are not fixed and can fluctuate. If a tenant can neither pay the monthly charges nor sell his apartment, he may have to surrender his shares to the corporation. It might then be necessary to increase the assessments on the remaining tenants to pay the carrying charges for the empty apartment. During the depression of the 1930s some cooperative apartment owners lost their investments because a dwindling number of tenants could not afford to operate a half empty building. In addition, the cooperative owner lacks the freedom of the sole owner. To make alterations in his apartment, he may be required to obtain the approval of the cooperative's board of directors. Usually he cannot sell or assign an interest in his apartment without the board's approval.

The cooperative owner gets a personal tax deduction for his share of the taxes paid by the corporation.

The condominium owner is the sole owner of his apartment, and he pays his own taxes. He can obtain a mortgage to buy it or later mortgage his apartment. He and other

Average Sales Price
Of New One-Family Houses

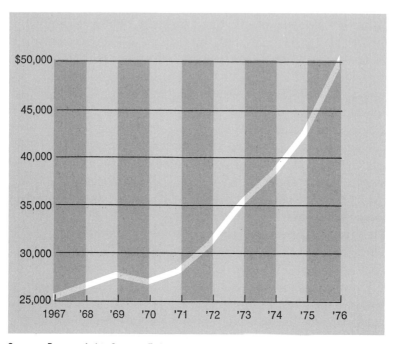

Sources: Bureau of the Census, Federal Reserve Board, Federal Home Loan Bank Board

residents of the project jointly own the land and common parts of the building, such as halls and stairways. Each resident pays an equal share toward maintaining common facilities. The major advantage of a condominium is that the owner cannot be assessed for the upkeep of empty apartments. The condominium owner may need the consent of other owners in the project to the sale of his apartment, but usually he has more freedom in choosing a purchaser than a cooperative tenant.

Condominium projects can be composed of town houses as well as apartments. This type construction is increasing in popularity as urban areas grow. Where land is expensive, the town house offers the charm of a private home at a reasonable price because more units can be built per acre.

Other real estate investments

As an investment, a home has its limitations. The prospects for profit are not the only consideration. You must consider your family's well-being and preferences. Alterations you make to your home for your family's convenience do not necessarily increase its market value. Many people live in rental apartments and use their capital to buy real estate exclusively for its profit potential. More people start by buying their own home. Home ownership gives them a basic course in real estate values and property management, and they acquire the confidence to expand their holdings. The question is whether real estate is the wisest investment for you.

With the nation's ever-increasing population, land values have increased enormously. Many a millionaire has made his fortune in real estate. Others have gone bankrupt. The wise and the fortunate bought farm land surrounding metropolitan centers and profited when it was subdivided for construction of houses sought by families fleeing the cities. Creeping decay in the cities reduced the fortunes of many urban real estate owners.

Real estate investments usually require more capital than other types of investment. When you buy real estate, you should be prepared to hold it for a period of years. If necessary, you probably could sell your stocks or bonds in five minutes. It could take weeks or months to find a buyer for property. Before purchasing real estate, you should have resources enough so that some emergency will not force you to sell at a loss to the first buyer who comes along.

On the other side of the coin, real estate generally offers both a high rate of return on your investment and excellent opportunities for capital growth. An annual income of 10 to 15 percent of your investment is not uncommon for real estate holdings. Property values have been known to double in a few years.

Some real estate investments afford tax advantages because of depreciation allowances for buildings. Since rentals and values move with the economy, the real estate investor also has protection against the eroding effects of inflation.

A word of advice here: Before you buy real estate, investigate thoroughly.

There are three basic ways of getting information and advice on real estate investments.

First, consult a reliable real estate broker. Take pains to seek out a well-established broker with a good reputation. The majority of real estate brokers are straightforward and ethical and have the best interests of their clients at heart. A few are concerned only with making a sale and getting the commission.

Second, you should become knowledgeable about real estate values and the legal and financial aspect of real estate investments. You can do this by reading real estate sections of newspapers, books, and other publications, and by talking to brokers, bankers and property owners.

Third, and perhaps most important, don't sign a contract until you have checked the details. If, for example, you are considering the purchase of a service station, you should look over the property, ask the present lease holder whether he intends to stay and check with the mortgage holder to make certain you encounter no problems there.

With these points in mind, let's examine some types of real estate investments:

There has been increasing speculation in unimproved real estate. Vacant land may be purchased not to improve it but for the purpose of resale at a profit some time in the future. You usually get no income from unimproved real estate. Except for the deduction for mortgage interest and taxes, you get no tax savings since land itself does not qualify for a depreciation allowance. When you buy unimproved real estate, be prepared to conduct a holding operation until it increases in value. This is risk investment, and it usually is a long-term investment.

Picking the right location is the key to success in investing in unimproved real estate. The wise investor carefully examines shifts in population. On a national scale, the population is moving to the West and Southwest. Real estate in these areas is increasing in value as more and more industrial development occurs. But there also is potentially valuable land in the densely populated states of the Northeast as the suburbs expand into open country. The investor should study the growth patterns of cities and states before deciding where to buy unimproved real estate. If a community is growing rapidly toward the south along a main expressway, but very slowly or not at all to the north, then the prospect for profit obviously is greater south of the city.

Each year, more people have more leisure time. Thus, land in recreation and vacation areas could prove an investment opportunity. This could be unimproved real estate near beaches, lakes or winter sport areas. Property in these sometimes thinly populated areas has an extra advantage: Taxes generally are low since the community has not provided schools, fire protection, and roads. But remember that taxes will rise as these facilities are added.

Investments in vacant land require little of the investor's time. There are few maintenance problems and no rent to collect from tenants.

Investments in improved real estate—whether it is a parking lot or an office building—are another matter. Besides money, they may require time plus experience in property management. For the part-time investor, the answer may be some kind of participating interest in investments in improved real estate.

Here are some of the ways this can be accomplished:

Partnership: Suppose you want to buy an apartment building. You have the money to make the purchase, but you are concerned about management of the building. One solution would be to find a partner—someone you trust who has real estate management experience. By pooling your capital and his experience, you will have a better chance of success.

Syndicate: This essentially is a partnership in which a large number of investors pool their funds for large-scale investment. Syndicates occasionally limit their investments to special types of real estate or to certain geographic areas. For example, a syndicate might be formed to build apartment complexes in urban areas. Or it might be established to develop a winter resort area many miles from a city. Most syndicates are concerned only with single properties, but others are widely diversified in type of operation or investment. The person who participates in a syndicate owns a fractional share of the total syndicate investment. Usually he is a limited partner, not personally liable beyond his own interest for the debts and liabilities of the syndicate. In other words, if an investor buys a 10 percent share in the syndicate, he is liable for 10 percent of the syndicate's debts, but no more.

Because income tax deductions for depreciation, mortgage interest, and property taxes can be substantial, a syndicate often enjoys a high rate of return. There are, however, some drawbacks too. When the syndicate is doing well, the investor usually has little difficulty finding a buyer for his interest. But in bad times, he may run into trouble if he wants to sell his interest. A potential investor should make a careful investigation before putting his money into a syndicate. In some cases, marginal properties have been syndicated at inflated values.

Real estate corporation: The real estate corporation, like the syndicate, is in the business of buying, selling and owning real estate. The risk of investing in a corporation is less than investing in a syndicate. So is the return. A corporation is created by law and has an existence all its own. The shareholder is not responsible for any of its debts. But with incorporation, the income from the business becomes subject to double taxation. First, the profits of the corporation, itself, are taxed. Second, dividends are taxed when they reach the hands of stockholders. The tax cuts into profits, but the bite is overcome in part by the corporation's deductions for depreciation, property taxes, interest, and operating expenses, although profits are also reduced by these costs.

Stock in a real estate corporation, like any other corporate stock, is traded on exchanges or in the open market. Usually, it can be sold easily at the prevailing quoted price. In the language of the market, it has greater "liquidity" than other real estate investments. It is liquid; it flows easily from purchaser to buyer. The prices of real estate stock tend to move with general market trends, offering a hedge against inflation.

Real estate investment trusts: The investment trust is somewhat similar to a corporation, except it is managed by trustees, and the investors are known as beneficiaries. The big difference is in tax treatment. The income of the trust which is distributed is taxed only once. To qualify for its preferred tax treatment, there must be at least 100 beneficiaries (investors). More than 50 percent of the trust cannot be owned by fewer than six persons.

Common stocks

Common stock is basic to all corporate business. In fact, it has been called the cornerstone of the free enterprise system. If you own a share of common stock in a corporation, you own part of that corporation. You and the other stockholders own the company in common. You share the risks of ownership. If the company is profitable, you share in those profits. If the company fails, you lose your money.

The first common stock of a company doing business in North American was issued under a corporate charter granted by King Charles II of England to "the governor and company of adventurers of England trading into Hud-

How Land Values Are Rising

(As Shown by Average Prices of Farmland Per Acre)

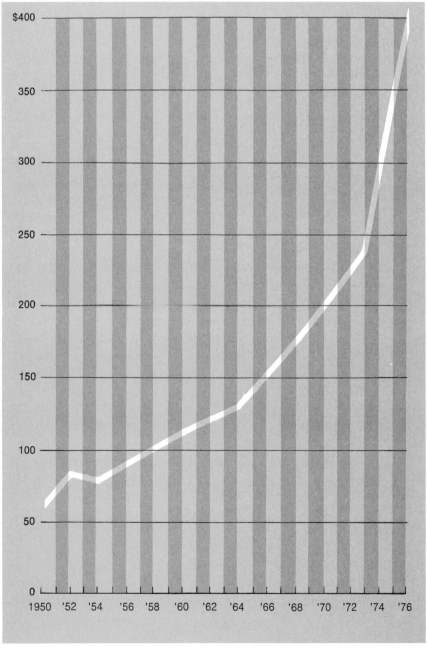

Source: U.S. Department of Agriculture

son's Bay." But there wasn't much interest in this first batch of common stock. In fact, it took many years for the idea of buying and selling common stock to catch on in America. Few people in the early years of the country had any surplus money for investment, and there were few industries requiring mass amounts of capital.

But times changed. Today, common stock is perhaps the most popular of investments. More than twenty-five million persons own common stock outright and there are nearly nine million shareholder accounts. Many millions of others have an indirect interest in common stock through their pension plans, savings accounts and insurance policies.

Why the popularity of common stock?

One reason is that, of all investments, common stock offers perhaps the greatest profit potential. One classic illustration: If you had bought 100 shares of stock in International Business Machines for $2,750 in 1914 and held on to it, your original 100 shares would have grown during the next half-century to nearly 28,500 shares with a market value of nearly $10 million.

While this may be an exceptional case, thousands of investors have made fortunes by putting money into the stock of growing companies in their early stages. But many others have lost money when a promising stock suddenly took a nose-dive. This points up one fact an investor should keep in mind: Common stocks, while they provide the greatest profit potential, also carry the greatest risk of loss.

Even the best common stocks will vary 25 to 30 percent in price in a normal year. While government regulation has curbed the practices which contributed to the great stock market crash of 1929, economic conditions have a strong effect on stock prices. A depression or recession can send stock prices tumbling. On the other hand, because common stocks follow general economic trends, they can provide a hedge against inflation. When the nation's economy is on the upswing, stock prices generally are on the upswing, too.

This protects the purchasing power of the dollars invested in common stock.

How and why is common stock sold?

Here is an illustration:

James D. Dandy, electrical engineer, invented a new type burglar alarm and had it patented. A rising crime rate convinced him there was a ready market for it. He had $5,000. He needed $20,000 more to rent a small building, buy equipment, hire workers to produce the alarm and salesmen to market it. His bank refused to lend him the money. Banks use their depositors' money cautiously and usually make loans only to established businesses. So he decided to form a company, the Jim Dandy Burglar Alarm Co., and sell shares in the company to raise the capital needed. Dandy and four friends formed a corporation, and each put $5,000 into it. As evidence of joint ownership, each received a stock certificate for one share of stock in the corporation.

Business boomed. The company soon needed a larger plant and more machinery to fill the orders for the burglar alarm. To raise the money, the company issued five more shares of stock. Five more investors paid $7,000 a share. A share of stock now was worth more than before because the company was a going concern with a ready market. This sale added $35,000 in capital to the original investment of $25,000. The original investors, who began as sole owners of a company capitalized at $25,000, now owned half a company capitalized at $60,000. Each had made a paper profit of $1,000. The new investors were not out any money. They were buying prospects for growth.

The company now had ten stockholders—ten part-owners. Since it would be difficult to run a business with ten bosses, they elected a board of directors to oversee the operations of the company. Jim Dandy was named president and operating head of the company. The directors gave the title of vice-president to his top assistant and appointed a treasurer. At regular intervals, these officers were required to report to the board of directors on the progress of the company. Once a year the board held a meeting open to all stockholders. At this meeting, the management made its annual report to the owners.

Because of the cost of starting a new business and expanding it, the investors received no income during the first two years of operation. But their progress interested others in purchasing stock. Their shares were growing in value. This was capital growth. The first earnings were plowed back into the business and increased the value of the shares. The third year the company reported profits of $10,000. Since all stockholders like dividends, and the board of directors knew it, the board decided to pay out $3,000 to investors. It declared a dividend of $300 per share. This was a return on investment of 6 percent for the first five investors and 4.3 percent for the second group of investors. The $7,000 reserved for expansion increased the basic value of a share of stock. The declaration of a dividend interested many people in buying stock.

No investor wanted to sell his entire holdings. But some were ready to take part of their profits. So the board of directors decided to split the stock 100 for one. The owner of every share of original stock exchanged his share for 100 shares of the new common stock. Each new share was worth one-hundredth as much as each old share. But then each stockholder now had 100 times as many shares as he started with. After the stock split, Jim Dandy Burglar Alarms had 1,000 shares of common stock outstanding.

One investor decided to sell half his stock, fifty shares. He visited a broker. The broker already had received inquiries about the stock, and he quickly arranged the sale of the shares. The part-owner selling his shares made a handsome profit. The corporation received none of the money. The only time a company gets any money for its stock is when it is first issued.

A "par value" is listed on many stock certificates. This value is set by the company when it issues the stock. It may be $1 or more. Unless you are buying into a brand new company, the par value has little relation to the current value of your stock. If a company prospers and expands over the years, its stock may sell for fifty times par. On the other hand, if a company lost half its property in a fire soon after it issued stock, a share with a "par value" of $10 might be worth only $5. Because par values can be misleading and often are misunderstood, many states allow a corporation to issue no-par stock. In such instances, the corporation's board of directors usually gives a "stated value" to each share. This stated value does not appear on the stock certificate.

There are more meaningful ways to describe the worth of a share of stock. These include book value and market value. The book value is determined by dividing the number of outstanding shares into the company's net assets. This is the amount of money a shareholder would receive if the business was closed and all creditors paid off. A stock's book value is of only passing concern to most investors, since they are interested in growing companies, not those about to go out of business.

The market value of a stock is the price the last buyer was willing to pay and the last seller was willing to accept. The market value is the price quoted in newspaper reports of stock market transactions. The price alone gives little indication of a stock's quality. You cannot tell from today's price what the price will be tomorrow.

The pattern of a stock's prices in recent weeks, months and years does give a clue to its quality. A stock whose market value has climbed steadily generally is a better buy then one whose market value has declined or fluctuated wildly.

Many experts say the most important measurement of a stock's worth are cash dividends and earnings. A company with a long record of paying substantial dividends is prized by investors seeking a steady income. The earnings, whether or not they are paid out in dividends, are important to all investors. Most companies report their per share earnings annually and even quarterly. This is the net income of the company divided by the number of shares outstanding. If a company had a net income of $1 million last year, and there were 100,000 shares outstanding, the per-share earnings would be $10.

If the stock were selling for $100, it would be selling at ten times earnings. In the language of the market, 10 is its price earnings ratio, meaning it is selling at ten times earnings, a conservative price. If the stock were selling for $300, it would be selling at thirty times earnings. The price earnings ratio would be 30, and that is a high price for a stock. People often buy stocks selling for as much as forty times earnings in anticipation of great and rapid growth. But any decline in earnings can cause such a stock to drop in price overnight.

If you are thinking about investing in the stock market, you also should know about stock rights. This is a right given stockholders to purchase additional shares in the company at a stated price. Let's assume the Jim Dandy Burglar Alarm Co. kept growing, and the board of directors decided after five years to issue more stock to raise money for expansion. As a bonus to existing stockholders, the board might decide to issue "rights certificates" to them. Each certificate would give the stockholder first opportunity to buy new stocks in proportion to the number of shares he already owns.

For example, if an investor had a 10 percent interest in a company, he would have the right to buy 10 percent of the new shares. Because the additional stock most often is offered to stockholders below the current per share market price, rights certificates have a market value of their own and are actively traded.

Rights certificates usually expire after a relatively short time. "Warrants," which also are options to buy securities at a certain price, usually are valid for years or even indefinitely. Warrants often are issued as inducements to buy other securities, such as bonds. They, too, are marketable; they can be bought and sold on the open market.

Preferred stocks

Business was good at Jim Dandy Burglar Alarms. The plant had been expanded, new machinery had been installed. Sales were growing. The company's assets now exceeded $200,000. Then the board of directors heard of a golden opportunity for further expansion. The Big Eye Co. was for sale. Located in the same town, the Big Eye Co. manufactured closed circuit television surveillance systems for use in plant and building protection. It was owned and operated by a single family. Its president had indicated he wanted to retire and invest whatever he got from the sale of the company in such a way as to yield him and his family a safe, reasonable income.

The directors of Jim Dandy Burglar Alarms were interested in acquiring the Big Eye Co. because it offered them a chance to move into a new area of protective services. But where could they get the $100,000 the owners of the Big Eye Co. had set as the price for the company?

The directors had no cash to offer, so they proposed this deal: Jim Dandy Burglar Alarms would take over the Big Eye Co. and pay for it by issuing *preferred stock* in Jim Dandy Burglar Alarms. An issue of 1,000 shares with a value of $100 per share would be given to the owners of the Big Eye Co. in exchange for their company.

The owners of the Big Eye Co. accepted the offer because, like most preferred stock, this issue would assure them a prior claim on all assets of Jim Dandy Burglar

Alarms, after all debts had been paid, should it ever be necessary to dissolve the company.

Preferred stock is a senior security. It ranks ahead of, or is senior to, other securities issued by the company—in this case, the company's common stock. In the event of liquidation, the holders of preferred stock would get their money before the holders of common stock got theirs.

Dividends on preferred stock usually are fixed at the time the stock is issued. The dividends commonly range from 4 percent up to 6 percent or 7 percent, with the higher dividends prevailing in periods when interest rates on borrowed money are high. The dividends must be paid to the holders of preferred stock before any dividends can be paid to owners of common stock. Preferred stock is a secure investment. But because the dividend is fixed, it cannot grow as rapidly in value as common stock can. A prosperous company may keep increasing its dividends to common stock holders, until the dividend per share of common stock is far greater than the dividend per share of preferred stock.

A company sometimes issues preferred stock in series, such as preferred A, B, and C, or Class A, B, and C, first preferred, second preferred, and so on. Dividends must be paid on the first in a series, such as Class A, before they can be paid on the second.

Preferred dividends can be cumulative or noncumulative. With cumulative preferred, if the company cannot pay the agreed-upon dividend in any year, the amount due for that year would be carried over and would be paid the following year or whenever the company had enough earnings to pay it. If the company could not make dividend payments on the preferred stock for a number of years, the dividends would continue to add up during all that time and would have to be paid in full before the common stockholders received any dividend payments. This would not be the case if the stock were noncumulative. The company would then

Financial Assets of Households
1946 and 1976

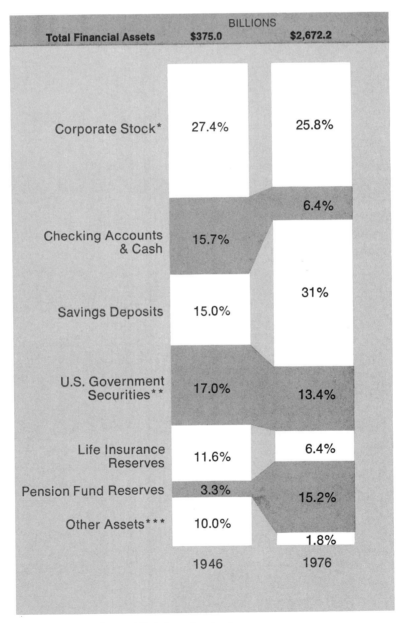

Total Financial Assets	BILLIONS $375.0	$2,672.2
Corporate Stock*	27.4%	25.8%
Checking Accounts & Cash	15.7%	6.4%
Savings Deposits	15.0%	31%
U.S. Government Securities**	17.0%	13.4%
Life Insurance Reserves	11.6%	6.4%
Pension Fund Reserves	3.3%	15.2%
Other Assets***	10.0%	1.8%
	1946	1976

*Includes mutual funds.   **Includes savings bonds.
***Includes state and local obligations, corporate bonds, mortgages, and miscellaneous.

Note: "Households" include personal trusts and nonprofit organizations.

Source: Federal Reserve Board

have no obligation to make up dividends missed because of insufficient income.

Preferred stock also can be classified as participating and nonparticipating. The nonparticipating variety is issued most often. Under it, the holders would not benefit, beyond the regular dividend, from any of the extra profits the company might earn. If business were so good that dividends on common stock were doubled, the holders of the preferred stock still would get nothing more than their specified dividend.

Another type of preferred stock, one that has become increasingly popular in recent years, is known as convertible preferred. It carries a provision allowing the owner to convert the preferred stock into a specified number of shares of common stock.

For example, if a company issued convertible preferred stock at a time when its common stock was quoted at $22 or $23 a share, the conversion clause might provide that every share of the new $100 preferred could be exchanged for four shares of the company's common stock at any time in the next five years. The exchange would be advantageous only if the price of a share of common stock climbed to more than $25 a share.

Convertible preferred stock has its advantages and disadvantages. If a company is successful and the price of its common stock rises, the convertible preferred stock will have a corresponding increase in value, since it can be exchanged for the common. But if the price of the company's common stock declines, the convertible preferred's value will suffer too.

Because it is tied to the common stock of a company, the price of convertible preferred stock generally fluctuates more than the price of the other preferred stocks. As stated earlier, dividend rates on most preferred stocks are set in advance. For this reason, they often are called fixed-income securities. So are corporate bonds.

Corporate bonds

A corporate bond is simply a paper certificate stating that the owner of the bond has loaned money to the corporation which issued the bond. The basic difference between stocks and bonds is this: A man who buys stock in a company actually owns part of that company. A man who buys a company's bond simply lends his money to the company. The stockholder expects to collect dividends on his stock and thus share in the company's profits. The bondholder expects only to earn a fixed return on his investment in the form of interest payments.

If a company succeeds, the stockholder could make a substantial profit because the price of his stock would go up. The bondholder knows that no matter how successful the company, the return on its bonds will remain the same. While the bondholder cannot expect to make a great profit, he runs less risk of losing his money. His investment is safer because bonds represent debts. If the company is dissolved, bondholders get their money first, before stockholders get a penny. But this does not mean that bonds are riskless. If a company fails, the bonds may not be paid off either.

Bonds offer corporations a way to raise money without issuing more stock, without further increasing the number of owners. They are properly used by well-established corporations seeking large sums of money no single bank would lend to one corporation.

The reason for buying a bond is to secure a safe haven for your money and an assured return. The investor has a choice of several types of bonds, including the following:

Debentures: The most common type of bond issued by large, well-known industrial firms. These are backed solely by the general credit of the corporation. No specific real estate or property is pledged as security for the bonds. A debenture has been aptly described as a "giant-size I.O.U."

Convertible bonds: There are many kinds on the market, and their terms vary widely. But all have this in common: They give the owner the privilege of converting his bond into a specified number of shares of the corporation's common stock. While convertible bonds offer the chance to make an extra profit if the stock rises, their guarantees of safety sometimes are not as great as other types of bonds.

Mortgage bonds: This type is secured by a mortgage on a specified piece of corporation property, such as the land on which a plant is built, or the plant building itself. If it is a first-mortgage bond, all of the company's property is pledged as security. These bonds generally are rated among the highest-grade security investments, since they give the investor the greatest possible safety—a first mortgage bond has first claim on earnings and assets. Mortgage bonds take precedence over all other company securities, including debentures.

Interest rates paid on bonds vary from company to company, and they are affected by general business conditions. In the 1920s, high-grade bonds were paying 6 percent interest or more. During World War II, top quality bonds were paying only $2\frac{1}{2}$ percent interest. Recently, interest rates again have climbed as high as 10 percent.

Bonds usually are issued in $1,000 denominations, with interest payable semi-annually.

Often, the interest rate of a bond is called the "coupon rate." This is because bonds traditionally were issued with coupons attached, each coupon representing semi-annual interest. These coupons were clipped when they came due and presented to the company's paying agent for payment of interest. (This is how the phrase "coupon clipper" came to denote a wealthy individual.) In recent years, more and more companies have done away with coupons. Instead they simply mail interest payments to the registered owners of the company's bonds.

The bond certificate states the interest rate and the maturity date. The maturity date is the date the company promises to redeem the bond. In general, the stronger the company, the longer the maturity time. A small company might issue ten-year bonds. A large company might issue thirty-year bonds. Some bonds, known as serial bonds, are paid off in annual installments instead of in a lump sum at maturity. Most bonds have "call" provisions which allow a company to redeem them before maturity and thus cut down on interest payments if it can.

The par value of a bond is the full face value of it and the price at which the company is committed to redeem it eventually. The market price can fall below par. A bond may be issued at a par value of $1,000 with an interest rate of 4 percent. You may pay more or less than $1,000 for it on the market. Your income from it remains the same, $40 per year. This is more than 4 percent on your investment if you purchased the bond in the market for $900. It is less than 4 percent on your investment if you purchased the bond in the market for $1,100. The interest rates offered by other institutions tend to affect the rise and fall of bond prices.

Bonds can vary widely in quality, and it is wise to check the ratings given them by several independent services, such as Moody's Investors Service or Standard and Poor's. Unless you know what you are doing, it is wise to stick to top quality bonds. The yield may be higher on speculative bonds, but the chances of losing money also are higher. Many investors buy corporate bonds because they are safer and more stable than common stocks. They do not, however, offer the hedge against inflation that common stocks do.

Government and municipal bonds

Perhaps the safest bonds of all are those issued by the United States Government. The reason: The Government's power to tax (and to raise money) stands behind them.

There are two basic types of securities issued by the

Federal Government: the nonmarketable and the marketable.

The most popular nonmarketable bonds are Series E and Series H United States savings bonds. They are owned by millions of Americans. Their advantages and disadvantages were discussed earlier.

Marketable securities are held primarily by financial institutions—banks and savings and loan associations, trust funds, pension funds, and some individuals in middle and upper-income brackets.

Some, called "Treasury bills," are issued for short periods of time, such as three months. Then there are "Treasury certificates," which mature within a year, and "Treasury notes," which may run for as long as five years. Interest rates on these issues at times have exceeded 8 percent.

"Treasury bonds" now outstanding have maturities running from five years to thirty-two years. New bonds can run any length of time. The yield on these bonds in recent years has ranged between 5 percent and 8 percent. Many billions of dollars in these bonds, known as "Treasurys," are now outstanding, and "Treasurys" worth millions of dollars are traded each day on the bond markets.

States, cities, and other local units of government—such as school districts and housing authorities—raise money to build schools, roads, hospitals, sewers, and other public projects by issuing "municipal bonds." Interest rates on municipal bonds in recent years have averaged about 6 percent, but some carry rates of 7 percent or more. Maturities range from a few years to as long as fifty years.

There are two kinds of municipal bonds—general obligations, which are backed by the taxing power and credit of the state, city, or other unit of government, and revenue bonds, which are secured by a pledge that revenues collected from the project being financed, such as a turnpike or water system, will go to pay the interest and principal.

Municipal bonds have special appeal to persons in high income brackets because the interest they yield is exempt from federal taxes. In addition, interest on municipal bonds usually is exempt from state taxes in the state where the bonds are issued. A man paying 50 percent of his income to the government in taxes would get as much from a municipal bond paying 3 percent interest as he would from a common stock paying a dividend of 6 percent.

These tax advantages should be weighed against some disadvantages to investing in municipal bonds. Many municipals are not as readily marketable as federal government or corporate bonds. If the owner needs money in a hurry, he may have to sell his municipal bonds at less than the price he paid for them. The investor who considers buying municipal bonds would be wise to consult specialists in these securities.

Experts recommend a balanced portfolio. The person with a modest nest egg can divide it, buying some securities for their safety features, others for income, and still others for capital growth. He also can make a single investment combining considerable safety with a fair return and some prospects for capital growth. No single security offers everything the investor wants. But every investor can achieve reasonable goals.

One of the most important single areas of fruitful investment is to be found in common stocks—the subject of the next chapter.

CHAPTER 4

Making Money in the Market

Among Americans, common stock is perhaps the most popular investment. Certainly it is the most enticing. Opportunities for capital growth are great. Prospects for income are substantial. The initial investment can be small. Stocks can be converted quickly into dollars. They do not demand the sort of supervision required by a family business or personal real estate holdings.

Yet anyone who can recall the stock market crash of 1929 knows the risks are high. Many who have invested since World War II have also suffered losses.

Can you afford to invest in the stock market?

Money management experts say a family can sensibly consider investing in securities when it can answer "yes" to these three questions:

1. Does the family have an emergency fund to tide it through a financial crisis?

2. Does it have sufficient life insurance to provide security for the family in the event of the breadwinner's death?

3. Does the family have money to invest it will not need for at least several years?

If you pass muster on these three points, then you might face the promises and perils of the stock market.

Fluctuations in the market are common. Big drops in prices still occur occasionally. Nevertheless, the stock market is a safer place to invest than it was a generation ago. The Securities and Exchange Commission has watched over the public sale of securities since 1934. The Federal Reserve Board today regulates the purchase of stock on borrowed money, a practice known as buying on "margin". In 1929, you could buy stock by putting up only 10 percent of the money it cost—$10 for $100 worth of stock. Of late, the margin requirement has been 50 percent, calling for a minimum of $50 cash to purchase $100 worth of stock. When a stock becomes too erratic, stock exchanges sometimes place purchases of an individual stock on a cash basis, no margin being allowed. When panic selling appears, the exchanges suspend trading.

The growing number of large institutional buyers, mutual funds, and insurance companies have an impact on the market. Though institutional investors are not apt to unload their huge holdings in panic, their buying and selling of large blocks of stock can have a major influence on stock prices.

Why are you investing?

To finance a child's college education ten years from now? To provide security when you retire in perhaps thirty-five years? To make certain that the estate you leave your family is adequate? You may have one goal or more. Once you know what you want, you can make a decision about what types of common stocks would serve your purpose.

Making the right investment is no easy task. There are about 4,000 different common stocks listed on the national and regional exchanges. Many more are traded on the over-the-counter market. And common stock is only one area of possible investment.

Investment experts usually separate common stocks into four broad categories:

1. *Growth stocks:* These usually are associated with expanding industries—electronics, communications, office equipment, publishing, airlines, aerospace. Many companies in these fields have doubled their sales in the past five years and are steadily moving into other markets. As a general rule, they plow the bulk of their earnings back into research and the development of new products. The per share earnings of some have increased 200 percent or more within the past decade, which explains why they are classified as "growth" stocks.

2. *Income stocks:* These generally have a good record of paying cash dividends. Usually listed in this category are stocks of established industrial or merchandising companies serving broad consumer markets—such as utilities, food chains, and natural resource companies, such as coal, copper, lead, and petroleum. The companies usually pay out 50 to 70 percent of their net earnings each year as dividends.

3. *Trading stocks:* These often are called cyclical stocks because they tend to follow economic cycles. Their earnings tend to fluctuate widely between boom and recession periods. For example, when building construction is going strong, cement, gypsum, lumber, and plumbing companies will be booming. But when construction falls off, the earnings and fortunes of building supply companies generally drop too.

Others often listed in this category are steel companies

Industrial Stock Dividends
And the Cost of Living, 1926-1976

(1926=100)

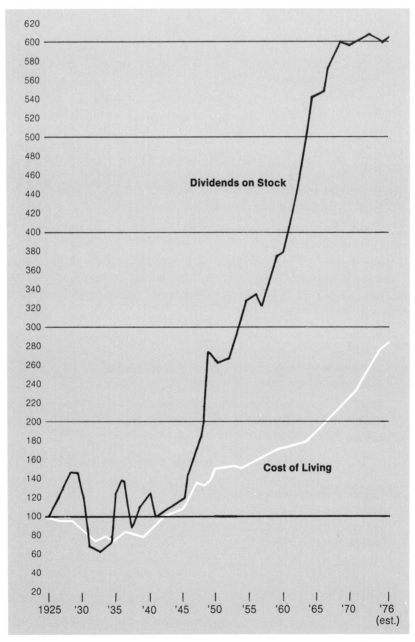

Source: Dividends of Standard & Poor's Industrial Stocks and the Bureau of Labor Statistics, U.S. Department of Labor, both on a 1926=100 base.

and automobile and truck manufacturers. Market prices for stocks tend to follow earnings, and the prices of these stocks reflect peaks and valleys in the demand for their products.

4. *Speculative stocks:* These usually are low-priced issues of unproven merit. They appeal to some investors because of the hope—however remote—that a small investment might suddenly turn into a fortune if the company strikes uranium or scores a scientific break-through.

What kind of stocks should you buy?

The answer, as indicated, depends on your goals.

A young couple with moderate income would like to see their few investment dollars multiply over the years until their children are ready for college or until they themselves are ready for retirement. Properly selected growth stocks might best suit their plan. But when they reach retirement, this same couple may desire to shift the emphasis of their investment program to achieve a steady income. This could be done by selling their growth stocks and buying income stocks.

What about persons of modest means who have relatively few years in which to accomplish their goals—a middle-aged couple planning retirement, or the parents of a twelve-year-old looking forward to college? These persons cannot afford the risk of highly speculative stocks. Yet, they must have some growth if they are to succeed. They might compromise by buying stocks combining moderate growth potential with stability.

If an investor is most concerned with preserving his capital to protect his retirement program for use in a few years, he would stress more stable stocks, foregoing part of the income and growth potential.

From the estate planning point of view, a degree of stability should be sought, perhaps combined with moderate growth potential. Remember, the basic objective of investing for estate purposes is the systematic build-up of capital over a long period of time.

Cyclical stocks appeal mostly to speculators who believe they can make money buying stock at a low price and selling it when the price goes up. Most experts say that families investing for the future should not attempt this "in and out" trading. These experts also recommend that investors seeking financial security steer clear of speculative stocks. But if the urge to take a fling at speculative issues overcomes you, they suggest you allocate only a small sum for risky purchases, bearing in mind that you may never see the money again.

Because no part-time investor can keep abreast of the thousands of stocks being bought and sold daily, money-management counselors say it is best to stick to the stocks of larger and better-known companies. If many people hold a certain stock, it is easier to buy and sell the stock on short notice.

As your investments grow, it is considered wise to seek diversification. If, for example, your first purchase was stock of a company in the communications industry, you may want to pick another industry, such as aerospace, for your second purchase. This gives you some protection for your invested capital. If the communications industry falls upon hard times and the value of its stock tumbles, you have a hedge because of your investment in the second industry.

Investors often are warned: "Don't put all your eggs in one basket."

They, in turn, ask: "How many baskets should we use?"

If you have less than $10,000, some experts advise against more than two or three different stocks. If you have up to $100,000, you might go to about six different stocks.

The number of "baskets" depends on how much money

you have to diversify and how much time you have to watch your "eggs."

Where to get information

No investor can expect to have first hand knowledge of all the thousands of stocks being sold today. He must rely on statistics and information prepared by others. The problem is in determining where to get reliable information.

The investor can start by reading a reputable financial newspaper or the financial pages of a large metropolitan newspaper. This will help him keep abreast of business trends in general and certain industries and companies in particular.

In addition to articles about current business developments, newspapers publish daily market quotations for stocks traded on the major exchanges. The stock listing for a hypothetical company might look like this in a newspaper table:

1		2	3	4	5	6	7	8
Year to Date		Stock &	Sales in					Net
High	Low	Dividend	100s	Open	High	Low	Close	Change
40½	36¾	XYZ 2	15	37¾	38½	37	38½	+ ½

Column 1 shows the total fluctuation in the price of the stock during the current year. The highest the price has been during the year is 40½, or $40.50 per share; the lowest 36¾, or $36.75.

Column 2 gives the name of the company, in this case the hypothetical XYZ Corporation, and the annual dividend, in this case $2.

Column 3 shows the total shares traded on a particular day, with two zeros omitted. The actual total this day was 1,500 shares.

Column 4 lists the price at which the first trade of the day was made. The 37¾ means $37.75 per share.

Column 5 lists the highest price paid for the stock of the XYZ Corp. on this particular day. The 38½ means $38.50 per share.

Column 6 reports the lowest price paid this day, $37 per share.

Column 7 registers the per share price of the last sale of the day. In this case, the last sale was the same as the highest sale, or $38.50 per share.

Column 8 records the difference between the closing price on this day (38½) and the closing price for the preceding day (38). The closing price on the preceding day may have been either higher or lower than the opening price this day.

Not all newspapers carry the full eight columns. Some omit the high and low for the year and the opening price of the day. Some list only the name of the security and the closing price.

At a glance you can get a complete picture of how the stock of XYZ Corporation moved during one trading day. It would be foolish to draw any positive conclusion about a stock on the basis of one day's trading. But if you watch a stock over a period of time and compare it closely with a dozen or so others, especially in the same or in a related field, you will see how that stock is regarded by the thousands of people whose transactions from day to day make up the market.

Before you actually make any investments, you can gain experience without risking your money. This can be done by making "paper investments." Select some stocks and pretend you have purchased them. Record the purchase price, then each day read the market tables in your daily newspaper to see how your imaginary investments are doing. If the stocks you chose for imaginary investments make substantial gains, you may berate yourself for not actually having bought them. But what if it had been the other way around?

What if the stocks had lost instead of gained?

Charting these paper investments can become a game, perhaps pitting husband against wife in a friendly contest to see who can pick the best stocks. At the same time, both husband and wife would be gaining some experience with the market.

Besides the prices on individual stocks, most daily newspapers publish one or more reports on the average price of stocks on the different exchanges. There are a number of these "averages." Probably the best-known is the Dow Jones Stock Averages. The Dow Jones report actually gives four averages—one for industrials, one for transportation, one for utilities, and a composite intended to reflect conditions in all parts of the market. The transportation index is an average of prices for 20 transportation stocks. The utility index covers 15 utilities. The industrial average is based on the stocks of 30 leading manufacturers and distributors. The composite index includes all 65 stocks.

In recent years, other indexes have gained wide usage. One of these is Standard and Poor's. It too actually consists of four averages—one based on 425 industrials, another covering 15 railroads, a third based on 60 utilities, and a composite index including all 500 stocks.

A few years ago, the New York Stock Exchange began publishing its own official index. It covers all common stocks on the exchange, and besides a composite average includes separate figures on industrials, transportation stocks, utilities, and finance.

For a broader picture of what's happening in business, an investor can subscribe to one or more of the country's financial periodicals. Some of these magazines specialize in looking at the business situation primarily in terms of stock market values.

The New York Stock Exchange publishes a monthly magazine, called "The Exchange," and the American Stock Exchange publishes one known as the "American Investor." Both publish articles of general interest to investors.

For the investor who wants to keep posted on the nation's economy and current business conditions, there are some low-cost government publications. These include the monthly "Economic Indicators," prepared by the Council of Economic Advisors; the "Survey of Current Business," issued monthly by the Commerce Department; and another Commerce Department publication, "Business Cycle Developments," which focuses on key indicators that often point the way the nation's economic cycle is going. Still another government source of information is the Federal Reserve Board's monthly "Bulletin."

To get information on a specific company, you can consult one or more investors' manuals. In these massive volumes you will find a brief history of nearly every publicly owned company in the United States and detailed financial information on each—sales, assets, income, earnings, dividends, and stock prices. Two of the reference books found most often in broker's offices and in public libraries are Standard and Poor's "Corporation Records" and Moody's "Manuals."

These reference books don't give advice. But there are dozens of "investment advisory services" that do—at a price. Many of these services try conscientiously to provide solid advice, but a few have been in hot water with government agencies for advertisements promising pie-in-the-sky. One way to find out the name of a reliable advisory service is to go to a reputable brokerage office and see what service it takes.

How to choose a broker

There are no hard and fast rules to follow in selecting a broker, but experts in the investment field do offer some suggestions:

Ask trusted friends, perhaps a banker or lawyer, to recommend a broker. Then do a little checking yourself. Talk to some of the broker's clients. Visit the brokerage house.

Ask about the firm's research and its ability to provide you with reports on potential investments.

Become acquainted with the broker himself, who sometimes is called an "account man" or a "customer's man." For some investors, it is important to know and get along well with the broker. For others, it is enough to respect the broker's competence. Take your time in making a selection. You might want to do a little "comparison shopping." Visit another brokerage house. Talk to other brokers. Then when you are ready to make your selection, you will have confidence that you have picked the right man.

The New York Stock Exchange urges investors to seek out a firm that belongs to the exchange. Member firms must obey the exchange's rules and regulations.

There are many reputable firms which are not members of the New York Stock Exchange. In considering one, it might be wise to determine whether the firm is a member of the National Association of Securities Dealers. This quasi-official body has the authority to discipline member firms which violate its rules and regulations on trading procedures, commission rates, and other practices.

Many firms, knowing that big customers are few and far between, have rolled out the red carpet for small investors. You should expect your broker to answer any reasonable questions you might have. Don't expect him to spend hours with you discussing a small investment. He has other customers who need attention. And don't expect your broker to help you decide whether you should invest at all. You must make that decision yourself before you enter his office. There's another "don't": Don't expect the broker to know whether the market in general or some stock in particular is going to go up or down. No one knows the answer to that question. At best your broker can only supply an informed prediction.

There is nothing mysterious or exclusive about a brokerage house. A broker, like a banker, sells a financial service.

Like the banker, the broker often will give advice when asked. But giving advice is not his basic business. His business is to provide the machinery for buying and selling securities. In a sense, he is like a storekeeper who hands you the particular product you want to buy.

The affluent investor—the one with $100,000 or more to invest—can turn his money over to an investment counselor, prepared to make all the buying and selling decisions for the customer and see that they are properly executed by a brokerage firm. In New York City alone, there are more than 100 of these counseling firms. Their services are not free. They collect a fee, generally about 1 percent annually on the capital entrusted to them.

How a stock exchange works

The New York Stock Exchange is in a big, old building at the corner of Wall and Broad streets in Manhattan's crowded financial district. Inside it looks somewhat like an armory, with high ceilings and a trading floor about half the size of a football field.

Around the edge of the floor are rows of booths, open at both ends. They traditionally are called "telephone booths," but they bear no resemblance to the telephone booth you find on the street corner. Inside these booths are a dozen or more clerks, representing various brokers. They stand at a narrow shelf, where they do their paperwork. Within reach are either telephones or teletype machines linking the clerk with his home and branch offices.

Also on the exchange floor are eighteen trading posts— twelve on the main floor and six in an annex. These are horseshoe-shaped counters about ten feet by ten feet. Behind each counter work another dozen or so clerks. All stock transactions are conducted around the outside of the trading post. Above the counter are signs showing which stocks are sold at each post. Below each sign is a price indicator showing the last price at which a transaction in that stock took place. If the last price represented an increase, a "plus" mark is displayed. If it represented a decrease, a "minus" sign is shown.

What takes place on the floor when you place an order with your brokerage firm for 100 shares of stock? The brokerage firm relays an order by telephone or teletype to the clerk in its booth on the exchange floor. The clerk jots it down and hands it to his "floor broker" to execute. If the floor broker is not at the booth, the clerk can summon him by pushing a button. Each broker has a number, and when the clerk pushes the button, the broker's number is flashed on a large board at each end of the trading floor. If the broker is busy with other orders, the clerk can call upon men known as "two-dollar brokers." These men—there are more than 100 in all—earn their livelihood by transacting business for a number of different brokerage firms. The "two-dollar broker" got his name in the days when he received that fee for every order he executed. Nowadays, he receives a fee ranging from 50 cents to $4 per 100-share order he handles. His average fee per transaction is about $3. This fee is called a "floor give-up commission" because the broker who is responsible for the order gives up a part of his commission to the broker who actually executes the order.

Suppose you ordered your broker to buy 100 shares of Electronics Inc. As soon as the floor broker has your written market order to buy, he walks—no running is permitted on the exchange floor—to the trading post where the stock is traded. There he knows he will find many other brokers who might have orders to buy or sell Electronics Inc. As he approaches the post, he glances at the price indicated and finds that the last sale of Electronics Inc. was made for 15¾, or $15.75 a share. Someone might be willing to sell it for less than this price, so as your floor broker reaches the trading post, he simply asks, "How's Electronics Inc.?" He doesn't disclose yet whether he wants to buy or sell. Another broker may answer, "15⅜ to 15¾," or simply "Three-eighths to three-quarters." This means that 15⅜ is the most any broker is willing to pay to acquire the stock—known as the "bid"—and 15¾ is the lowest anyone holding the stock will sell it for—known as the "offer."

The broker with the order to buy naturally wants the cheapest price he can get, so he may make a bid: "One-half for 100." This means he will pay $15.50 a share for 100 shares. If no one responds, he may raise his bid by one-eighth of a point, the minimum fluctuation in the price of most stocks. Thus he would say, "Five-eighths for 100." A broker in the group with 100 shares to sell might at this point decide to accept the bid. If so, he says simply, "Sold." The transaction is sealed with that one word. No documents or money change hands at this time. The brokers involved in the transaction make notes and relay a report back to their offices. After the market closes for the day, the two brokerage firms involved will arrange for the actual transfer of the stock and the payment of the amount due for its purchase. This is done through a clearing house.

Stock exchange rules require that all bids to buy and all offers to sell must be made by open outcry. No secret transactions are allowed on the trading floor, and no broker is permitted to execute any orders except during the official trading hours of the exchange. When a sale takes place, it is noted by one of several exchange employees, known as "floor reporters," who are stationed outside each trading post. This reporter would make sure the price indicator for Electronics Inc. is changed from 15¾ to 15⅝, and that a minus sign is added to show the decline in price. Then he would mark a special precoded card, and insert it into an optical scanning device. The machine "reads" the name of the stock, the price and the number of shares transacted. This information goes through a computer, which relays it on to the "ticker tape" and, via leased wires, to the "tickers" in every broker's office in the country. Thus brokers everywhere learn of any stock transaction within minutes after it is completed.

Besides the New York Stock Exchange, called the "Big Board," there are some fifteen other stock exchanges in the United States. They differ somewhat in rules, regulations, and operating mechanics, but they function fundamentally the same way as the "Big Board."

The second largest exchange is the American Stock Exchange, located in a spacious new building in Manhattan.

The American Stock Exchange originally was known as the New York Curb Exchange because it actually operated as an outdoor, curbstone market until 1921, when it finally moved indoors. All of the major brokerage firms are among the more than 650 members of the American Exchange, which has about 1,200 listed stocks and normally handles about one-third the daily share volume of the New York Stock Exchange. As the average price of shares on the American Exchange is lower than that on the "Big Board," the American Exchange accounts for only about 20 percent of the total dollar value of sales on the New York Stock Exchange.

The third largest exchange is the Midwest Stock Exchange in Chicago. Other regional exchanges include the Pacific Coast Stock Exchange, located in both San Francisco and Los Angeles, the PBW Stock Exchange, Inc., and exchanges in Boston, Detroit, Pittsburgh, Cincinnati, Salt Lake City, and Spokane. All are registered with the Securities and Exchange Commission.

Originally, these regional exchanges were established to provide a market place for the stocks of local companies. As these companies grew and gained national reputations, they listed their stocks on exchanges in New York. In recent years, regional exchanges have begun to trade in the same securities listed on the New York exchanges. In fact, more than 85 percent of the business of regional exchanges today is in stocks listed on the "Big Board." So now, besides providing a market place for stock of local companies, regional exchanges handle some of the big name issues sought by investors everywhere.

Over-the-counter market

An estimated 50,000 companies offering securities to the public are not registered with any stock exchanges. The stocks and bonds they offer are bought and sold "over-the-counter." This is not a stock exchange. Rather, it is a way of doing business, a way of buying and selling unlisted securities. Instead of coming together face-to-face, as they do on the stock exchange floor, brokers deal with one another through a massive network of telephone and teletype wires that link thousands of securities firms here and abroad. These dealers range from the largest brokerage house on Wall Street to a one-man operation in a small town in the Midwest. The securities bought and sold in the over-the-counter market can range from a $2 per share stock in some little-known company to a $100 per share stock in a century-old blue chip corporation. But all transactions have one thing in common: The price is arrived at by negotiation—not by an auction system as on the exchange floor.

Here is how a typical over-the-counter transaction might take place:

Suppose you want to buy 100 shares of Computer Inc. The stock is not listed with any of the major regional exchanges, so you place an order with a securities dealer.

If the dealer has no Computer Inc. stock in the inventory of stocks he carries, he calls other dealers who have. He asks each the price at which they would sell 100 shares. Let's say the best price anyone quotes him is 12½, or $12.50 a share.

This is the "inside price," the price one dealer quotes another. Some dealers charge you this price plus a standard commission. Others quote you a price which allows them a profit. This is called the "outside price."

Whether he is buying or selling for you, the dealer takes a fee, either in the form of a commission on the transaction or a profit on it.

You need to know whether the price the dealer quotes you is fair.

A privately owned price reporting service, the National Quotation Bureau, publishes daily "pink sheets" listing the inside prices on thousands of over-the-counter stocks and bonds. These prices, collected from hundreds of dealers, have been a reasonably accurate indicator of the price a stock sells for.

The financial pages of many newspapers list the bid and asked quotations supplied by the National Association of Securities Dealers. These quotations do not represent actual transactions, but they are reliable reports of prices at which stocks can be bought and sold. The dealer's fee, be it markup or commission, is extra.

Bonds as well as stocks are sold over-the-counter. Virtually all government bonds traded in the open market are sold over-the-counter, either by banks or dealers specializing in this type of security. All municipal bonds and most corporate bonds are traded over-the-counter.

If a stock is new, if it is narrowly held, if it is not heavily traded, the chances are you will find it in the over-the-counter market. You will also find some old, established, and heavily traded stocks selling over-the-counter. The mammoth corporations, The American Telephone and Telegraph Company and General Motors, are traded on the New York Stock Exchange. But there is no clear distinction, no proper dividing line between stocks selling on major exchanges and stocks selling over-the-counter, between corporations which have joined an exchange and submitted to its rules and corporations which have not. The rule for all is the same: Investigate before you buy.

Two Ways to Make a Million

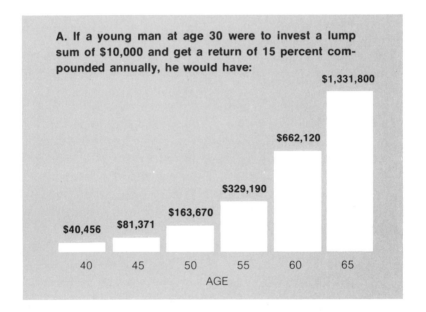

A. If a young man at age 30 were to invest a lump sum of $10,000 and get a return of 15 percent compounded annually, he would have:

$1,331,800

$662,120

$329,190

$163,670

$40,456 $81,371

AGE
40   45   50   55   60   65

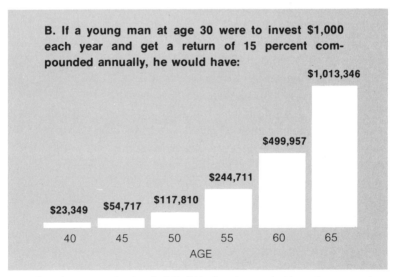

B. If a young man at age 30 were to invest $1,000 each year and get a return of 15 percent compounded annually, he would have:

$1,013,346

$499,957

$244,711

$117,810

$23,349 $54,717

AGE
40   45   50   55   60   65

Note: Examples assume reinvestment of all dividends and payment of taxes due on annual dividends from other income.

Source: Economic Unit, *U.S.News & World Report*

How to Become a Millionaire

The two examples on the facing page demonstrate the principle of "compound growth" in building your estate. In example A, an initial investment of $10,000 will snowball into $1,331,800 over a thirty-five year period, if the earnings of 15 percent are allowed to accumulate. In example B, a yearly investment of $1,000 over the same period of time will become $1,013,346 if the 15 percent return is reinvested annually. Both examples are based on an important assumption. It is that additional funds will be secured to meet any taxes which may be due on the earnings of these investments.

The 15 percent rate of return may sound high, but it is possible to achieve with many different types of investments. It might be realized in a carefully managed family business; and that rate of return is not uncommon in real estate that appreciates in value. According to statistics covering a recent twenty-year period, the combined annual return from dividends and capital appreciation on all common stocks averaged roughly 14 percent. Average returns for some types of stock were even higher, although returns on still other types were sharply lower. Some top-performing mutual funds also have shown a capital appreciation of more than 15 percent during a recent ten-year period, but this rate varies from fund to fund.

Although no one can predict with certainty the future growth of any investment, these figures suggest that you too might become a millionaire if you can manage to carry out these investment formulas.

When to buy

Once you have picked a stock, you face another big decision: When is the best time to buy? Some investors use all sorts of charts and market analyses in trying to answer this question. The average family man with a few dollars to spare probably doesn't have the time to indulge in such elaborate calculations. But there is a simpler, somewhat mechanical procedure people can use, especially those who invest only small sums periodically. It is called "dollar-cost averaging."

Here is how it works:

Suppose you have selected a common stock and decide you can invest $120 every three months. When you make your first purchase on January 1, the price is $10 per share. So you get 12 shares. (For reasons of simplicity, these calculations exclude commissions and other fees.)

When you make your second quarterly purchase, on April 1, the price per share has dropped to $6 per share. So your $120 buys 20 shares. The downward trend continues, and on July 1, the price per share is $4. You get 30 shares. It falls further, and is $2 per share when you make your October 1 purchase. This time you get 60 shares for your $120. Then the price starts climbing. It is $6 a share on January 1, so you get 20 shares. It is $8 a share on April 1, and you get 15 shares. Now, after six quarters, let's take a look at your investment program. The table on the opposite page illustrates your purchases.

The total amount invested in the six quarters was $720. This bought 157 shares. Your average cost per share was $4.59 ($720 divided by 157 shares). With the last market price of $8, your total investment would be worth $1,256. Thus you would show a capital gain of $536 on the $720 you invested.

For this approach to succeed, you must have the emotional stability and the confidence in your investment choice

Date of purchase	Amount invested	Price per share	Number of shares bought
Jan. 1	$120	$10	12
April 1	120	6	20
July 1	120	4	30
Oct. 1	120	2	60
Jan. 1	120	6	20
April 1	120	8	15

Total amount invested $720 *Total shares bought* 157

to make your purchases on schedule, even when the market is in a slump. It is during periods of price decline that you bring your average price per share down most sharply, because you can buy more shares with the same amount of money. But don't let your concern with dollar-cost averaging become so great that you forget to review your investments periodically. If the price of your stock soars to fantastic levels, you must study the wisdom of further purchase. If the price of your chosen stock goes steadily downhill, you must decide whether the long-term outlook remains good, or whether further investment would be throwing good money after bad.

Keep this in mind: Whatever your average share cost, your prime concern should be with what your total investment will be worth when you are ready to cash it in.

For example, if the price per share started at $10, then dropped to $6, $4, and $2, and stayed at $2 for two more purchases you would have purchased 242 shares for your $720 investment. But if you had to sell at this time, you would receive only $484 as the market price, for a capital loss of $236.

This example underscores the need for periodic review of your investment program. In a situation of consistent price erosion, you might decide to sell and put the salvaged cash into a stock with greater potential. Or you might simply stop buying and hold on to the shares you already have in hope the market price will improve.

Another major point to remember: Dollar-cost averaging is not a magic formula that takes all the worry out of investing. Rather, it is a stock purchase plan that takes some of the worry out of investment timing. The secret, investment counselors say, is to select a good stock and then faithfully make regular purchases whether per share prices climb or fall.

Guide to stock value

As every investor knows, the future movements in the stock market are unpredictable, even by the experts. While stock market averages are heading up, some individual stocks may be going down. The investor, then, should look for good value in stocks. There are yardsticks you can use in your search. One of the most-cited guides is the "price-earnings ratio," or P/E for short.

In brief, the P/E is the stock market price compared with the company's latest twelve-month earnings-per-share of stock outstanding. This figure can be found in several financial reference works in libraries and brokers' offices.

It is easy to calculate the price-earnings ratio. Simply determine a company's annual per-share earnings, then divide it into the market price of the stock. For example, a stock selling for $28 and earning $2 per share net (after taxes) has a P/E of 14.

There is a wide variation in price-earnings ratios. Some stocks may have P/Es of 30 or 50 or more. Others are quoted at 10 or below. During the first half of the decade of the 1970s the average annual price-earnings ratio of common stocks ranged from about 7 to more than 18.

Experts say that very low P/E ratios can indicate that the company is considered to have small growth prospects and a flat or even declining earnings trend. They also point out that stocks of companies in cyclical industries have

Price/Earnings Ratio and Dividend Yield
On Common Stocks

Ratio

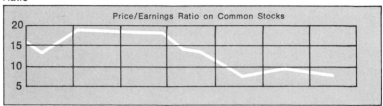

Percent

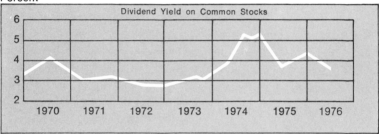

Sources: Standard & Poor's Corporation, Council of Economic Advisers

variable earnings and may have low P/E ratios. Such stocks
may or may not be good buys.

The goal of research-minded investors is to find stocks
with moderate P/E ratios and reasonably sound future prospects. The approach of investors interested in capital gains
will be different from that used by investors interested in
dividends. For example, older persons with a need for immediate income may be more interested in the dividend rate.
It is calculated by dividing the stock's market price into its
annual dividend. A stock selling at $40 and paying a $1.20
dividend would have a dividend rate, or yield, of 3 percent.

A high dividend rate does not necessarily mean good
value. The yield may be high because of a relatively high
"payout rate." Some corporations pay out as much as 70
percent of their earnings in dividends; others pay very little.
Growth companies tend to pay smaller dividends, preferring
instead to plow back earnings into research and expansion.

Investment costs: commissions and taxes

Your investment program will encounter two major expenses—sales commissions and taxes.

For many years, commissions were based on the number of shares involved in the transactions. This later was changed and the emphasis was placed on the money involved in the deal, with the commission percentage generally scaling downward as the amount of dollars increased.

In 1975 the Securities and Exchange Commission abolished a schedule of fixed fees which brokers could charge. This means that each broker is free to determine what fees to charge his customers. Since commissions may vary from broker to broker, experts suggest that you ask a broker what his commission schedule is before doing business with him. That way you will know in advance what to expect in the way of fees.

Some of your "income-producing expenses" can go toward reducing your tax bill. While a tax consultant can help you with specifics, the Internal Revenue Service offers these general guidelines:

"Fees you pay to a broker, a bank, or similar agent to collect your bond interest or dividends on shares of stock are deductible. But a fee you pay to a broker to acquire investment property, such as stocks or bonds, is not deductible. It is added to the cost of the property."

The IRS also advises:

"Investment counsel fees incurred in caring for your investments to the extent they relate to investments that produce taxable income . . . are deductible."

So, as you can see, the question of fees and taxes on income-producing property or investments is one you should consider ahead of time.

Since only members of the New York Stock Exchange can execute orders there, other dealers must route their orders for listed securities through some member for execution. This means you may have to pay an additional fee if you give an order to a nonmember, such as a bank or local securities dealer.

In addition to the fees you must pay to make investments, you can incur other costs in the form of specialized taxes. For instance, if you trade on an exchange based in New York, you must pay a small transfer tax whenever you sell a stock. This tax is not levied when you purchase a stock. The amount of the transfer tax varies according to the price of the stock sold. In addition to the transfer tax, a fee is levied on stock sales to cover the costs incurred by the Securities and Exchange Commission in its regulatory work.

You pay federal income taxes both on the income from investments and on profits from the sale or exchange of securities. There are many ways to keep your tax bill low, and it might pay you to consult a good tax adviser about your investment program. Don't wait until the end of the year to find out how much you owe the government. Tax planning can reduce your taxes and increase your capital.

The income you receive from investments, such as dividends and interest, generally is subject to the ordinary graduated income tax rates. You add investment income to salary and pay taxes on the total. There are two major exceptions to the rule.

An investor is allowed to exclude from income the first $100 in dividends received annually from domestic corporations. If the stock is jointly held in the names of husband and wife the exclusion is $200.

Second, interest on bonds issued by a state or any political subdivision of a state, such as a municipality, is exempt from federal income taxes.

Your profits from the sale of securities are known as capital gains, and losses from the sale of securities are called capital losses. The timing of the transaction makes an important difference from a tax standpoint. In 1976 and previously, if you bought a security and sold it within six months, you established a short-term capital gain or loss. This was taxed at the same rate as your ordinary income. But if you held the security for more than six months, you established a long-term capital gain or loss. This six-month requirement has been changed by Congress to nine months for 1977 and to one year effective in 1978.

Left unchanged by Congress is the taxation of long-term capital gains at just half the rate of short-term gains and income. For this reason, it often pays to hold a security longer than the specified period in order to receive the more favorable treatment granted long-term gains.

Tax experts say many investors overpay their taxes because they believe, incorrectly, that long-term capital gains are taxed at a flat 25 percent of the gain.

The government gives you a choice of two methods for calculating a long-term capital gain. You can deduct 50 percent of the gain from your gross income, then pay a tax on the balance at your ordinary income tax rate. Or you can pay a 25 percent tax on the total gain. Only taxpayers in the 50 percent income tax bracket can owe as much as 25 percent of their total profits to the government.

For instance, suppose you are a married couple filing a joint return with a taxable income—total income minus deductions—of $20,000 a year. You buy stock for $2,000 and sell it nine months later for $3,000. You have made a long-term capital gain of $1,000. Divide the $1,000 gain in half. Add the $500 to your other taxable income. Your top tax bracket is 28 percent. The tax due on your capital gain is $140. If you calculated your tax as a flat 25 percent of the entire capital gain of $1,000, the bill would be $250.

The maximum rate applies only to a single person with a taxable income as high as $38,000 or a married couple filing a joint return and reporting a taxable income as high as $52,000.

If you sustain a loss in the sale or exchange of capital assets, that loss is deducted from your capital gains before you figure your tax for the year.

If losses exceed gains in any one year, you can deduct a specified amount of the excess from your ordinary income. In 1976 and previous years, the maximum amount was $1,000; in 1977, $2,000; and beginning in 1978, $3,000. Any loss left over after this deduction can be carried forward into the next year.

The timing of your transactions can make a difference in your tax bill. Take the case of Mr. Jones, a bachelor with a taxable income of $12,000 in 1976. His top tax bracket was 27 percent. He bought ten shares of common stock for $1,000. Five months later he sold the ten shares for $2,000. He realized a short-term gain of $1,000. The tax due was $270—27 percent of $1,000. But suppose he had held the stock for seven months, then sold it at the same price. His tax on this long-term gain would have been $135, just half of the tax on a short-term gain.

Now let's look at an example of how losses can offset gains. Mr. Smith and his wife file a joint income tax return. Their taxable income is $16,000 a year, so their top tax bracket is 25 percent. They bought a stock and sold it in three months for a profit of $1,000. This is a short-term gain taxable at the same rate as their income, 25 percent, or $250. The same year they sell another stock they have held for only three months at a loss of $500. They deduct their $500 loss from their $1,000 gain. The net gain is $500. The second transaction reduces the tax owed to $125.

You should keep in mind, however, that the Internal Revenue Service does not allow a tax credit for losses in some instances. For example, loss deductions are not permitted on "wash sales," the sale of securities at a loss within thirty days before or after the purchase of substantially identical securities by the same person. Losses which result from sales between close relatives, such as husband and wife, are not allowed as tax deductions.

For everyone there is a limit to the game of keeping taxes low. You do not sell a stock to establish a small tax deduction if you can make a large profit by holding it. You do not hold on to a security to avoid a capital gains tax when you have an opportunity to switch to a much more profitable investment. The wise investor will watch his estate grow and see his taxes increase with his wealth.

We have seen that the way to invest successfully in common stocks is first to build an emergency fund, then prepare to invest surplus capital you won't be needing for several years.

Selecting a quality stock takes research. Your broker is one source of information. But he cannot make your decisions for you. The right stock for you depends on your needs and goals. No stock promises everything. A stock paying a high dividend is suitable for an investor in a low income tax bracket who needs income now. A growth stock paying no dividend at all may suit the purposes of an investor in a high income tax bracket building an estate to protect his family and allow him to retire.

The New York Stock Exchange is the world's largest securities exchange. You also can buy stock on the American Stock Exchange, at regional exchanges, and in the over-the-counter market. It is not where you buy but what you buy that matters.

The technique known as "dollar-cost averaging" can take some of the worry out of investment timing. For this approach to succeed, you should make a careful study before selecting a stock. Then you must make your purchases on a set schedule, such as once a month, no matter whether the stock is going up or coming down in price.

Tax planning can reduce your tax bill. Just don't let an obsession with taxes distract you from the job of planning a profitable investment program and building your estate.

You do not have to go it alone. Building an estate need not be a lonely, unassisted task. Investment clubs and mutual funds offer increasingly popular ways of joining a group in order to spread the risk and to command a broader range of investment than an individual could secure by himself.

Chances of gaining a better return for dollars invested is another attraction. If you are figuring the return on an investment over the short run, the difference of a few percentage points may not seem much. But if you are looking at longer term results, the differences can be surprising. Note the following table, based on annual compounding:

If you invest $10,000 at 5% for:	It will be worth:	But just a 1% greater return will add:	For a new total of:	Thus, your capital is increased an extra:
10 years	$16,289	$1,619	$17,908	9.9%
15 years	$20,789	$3,177	$23,966	15.3%
20 years	$26,533	$5,538	$32,071	20.9%
25 years	$33,864	$9,055	$42,919	26.7%

(Source: Brevits, No. 5, 1972, issued by Vance, Sanders & Co.)

As you can see from these figures, one percentage point assumes an impressive size over the long term.

Investment clubs

A typical investment club is composed of a dozen or so friends, neighbors, or business associates who meet once a month, put $10 or more each into a common pool, then spend an hour or two discussing the best possible investment for their money. The group decides what to purchase and when to make changes in their investments.

There are over 60,000 investment clubs in the United States with more than 800,000 members. Total assets of these clubs top $750 million, or an average of $15,000 per club.

A survey several years ago by the National Association of Investment Clubs, a non-profit organization, showed that 96 percent of the clubs are profitable. Almost 13 percent of the clubs surveyed reported returns of more than 25 percent compounded annually. The average annual earnings were 16 percent, nearly three times the rate of the 425 industrial stocks used in the Standard and Poor's average.

The age of the clubs was not necessarily a success factor. The top performer of the clubs studied was the Faculty Investment Club of Sandusky, Ohio. Although it was only two years old, it had an amazing 241 percent return compounded annually. Longer-established clubs do well, too. The oldest club surveyed, Mutual Investment of Detroit, had averaged a 15.4 percent return compounded annually since it was founded in 1940.

The stock market was once considered the domain of men. But no longer. More than one-fourth of the members of the National Association of Investment Clubs are women. These women had an average return of 14.64 percent. The men did slightly better. Their average return was 15.59 percent.

These statistics notwithstanding, financial counselors warn that unless an investment club follows some basic rules, its members can lose money in this era of speculation and market ups and downs.

It usually is best to limit the initial size of an investment club to ten or fifteen members. The club should be viewed as a long-term proposition. Members should get along well personally and also should agree on the basic approach to investing. All members should understand from the outset that an investment club is not the road to instant riches. A get-rich-quick philosophy can be a club's downfall.

Experts recommend that the club set a reasonable goal for growth of investments, including dividends and capital appreciation. Some of these authorities suggest a reasonable goal would be 10 percent growth a year. Others say 100 percent appreciation of investments within five years could be a target to shoot for.

Some basic rules:

—Invest a given sum, such as $10 or $20 per member each month—regardless of the level of the stock market or the general business outlook. By buying shares of a selected company at both higher and lower prices, you average out the per share cost in the long run.

—Dividends can be reinvested as they are issued. This gives the same snowballing effect as compound interest.

—Stick to common stocks of sound growth companies, but aim for a diversified portfolio. For example, shares in ten different corporations would be a protection against major swings in one segment of the economy or another.

Brokers usually are happy to accept a club account and give some organizational help, but a club should do its own stock selecting to gain experience. The difference between a successful and an unsuccessful club often can be traced to the amount of research and self-education members are willing to do and share with each other.

When an investment club is organized, an agreement should be drawn covering the club's investment policy, the maximum share any one member may own, how financial records will be kept, which member will deal with the club's broker, and how information will be gathered on prospective investments.

It might be wise also to consult a qualified lawyer or tax advisor before establishing a club. He can recommend ways of getting the biggest tax advantage for the club.

More information on how to form an investment club can be obtained by writing the National Association of Investment Clubs, 1515 E. 11 Mile Road, Royal Oak, Michigan.

Mutual funds

Some persons interested in investing in securities may

not have the time or inclination to make a detailed study of the stock market. A mutual fund may be the answer for them.

Mutual funds are like investment clubs in some respects. Money contributed by members is pooled for investments in stocks and bonds. But there are two big differences between investment clubs and mutual funds. First, an investment club has only a dozen or so members, while thousands of investors may participate in a mutual fund. Second, mutual funds have professional management. Experts do the buying and selling of stocks and bonds.

Mutual funds offer another advantage—instant diversification. Whereas a single stock will rise or fall with the fortunes of the company that issued it, mutual funds reflect the fortunes of many companies. The money contributed by fund participants is spread among fifty to one hundred different securities at one time, offering a much broader diversification than most investors could expect to achieve on their own.

When you join a mutual fund, you become the owner of a percentage of all shares in the fund. The number of shares you own depends on how much money you invest. Mutual funds derive their income from dividends on stocks and interest on bonds held by the fund, as well as from capital gains made when the experts buy and sell stocks. Statistics indicate these experts know their business. In a recent ten-year period, when stock prices were on the upswing, an investment of $10,000 in the average fund would have grown to $26,211 and produced dividends of $4,122.

You should be aware, however, that when the market shows a sharp decline, this is often reflected in many mutual funds. During the 1970s, for example, the assets of mutual funds dropped from a high of nearly $60 billion to about $35 billion in a five-year period. There also was a smaller decline in the number of shareholder accounts, to a total of about ten million such accounts.

How Mutual Funds Have Fared

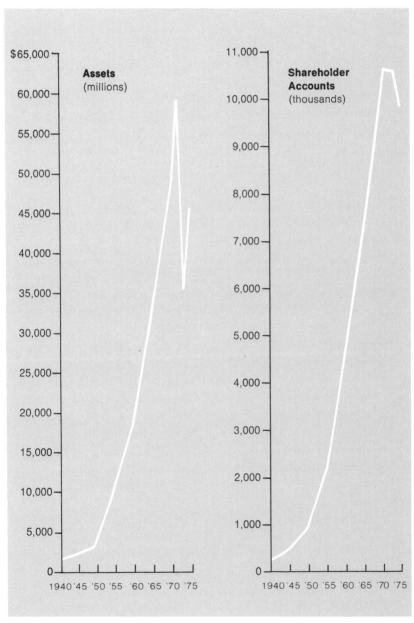

Assets
(millions)

**Shareholder
Accounts**
(thousands)

Source: Investment Company Institute

Mutual funds sometimes are called "open-end investment companies." This is because the number of shares in the fund changes from day to day. As new money is received from investors, new shares are issued. If an investor wants to drop out of a mutual fund, he usually can sell his shares back to the fund.

Don't confuse mutual funds with "closed-end investment companies." The latter issue a fixed number of shares when they are established, and the shares are traded on the market like any common stock. Before you can buy into a closed-end investment company, someone must be willing to sell his shares. And before you can get out, someone must be willing to buy your shares.

Not all mutual funds are alike. Some stress capital appreciation and are known as growth funds. Others seek to provide maximum dividends for their customers and are known as income funds. Still others try to strike a happy medium between growth and income. Generally mutual funds can be divided into three classifications according to the types of securities in their portfolios.

Common stock funds emphasize common stocks, but their portfolios may include some bonds and preferred stock. Usually, however, the investments in bonds and preferred stock will be small—less than 20 percent on the average. Because common stock funds follow closely the ups and downs of the stock market, they perhaps are best suited for investors who can tolerate the risk of fluctuations in income from the fund. Dividends are by no means assured, although the general record is good for steady quarterly payments.

A second classification is the balanced fund. This fund has bonds, preferred stock, and common stock in its portfolio, and tries to provide a consistent and relatively stable dividend. This usually is accomplished by sacrificing some opportunity for growth. Balanced funds tend to react slowly to an upswing in the stock market, but they generally protect the investor more in a declining market than does a common stock fund. Balanced funds have a record of consistent dividends.

Bonds and preferred stock funds, as the name indicates, place their investments almost entirely in bonds and preferred stocks. For this reason, growth potential is small. But the investor has good protection against recessions, and he has maximum security for his money. The dividend return usually averages from 3 percent to 7 percent.

The professional management of a mutual fund does not come free. Individuals purchasing shares in a mutual fund usually pay a fee known as an "acquisition charge" or "loading charge." There are a few funds that do not charge this fee. These are known as "no load" funds. But most funds charge a fee of about 8 percent. Part of the fee goes to pay the cost of paper work involved in handling the purchase, but the biggest portion goes for commissions to mutual fund salesmen. In addition to the acquisition charge, mutual fund officials receive an annual management fee usually amounting to about one half of 1 percent of the average net assets value of the fund.

There are three basic ways to invest in mutual funds:

1. *One-Time Purchase:* As the name implies, the investor places a lump sum into the purchase of mutual fund shares. He can increase or reduce his holdings any time he wants. The cost to the investor is the acquisition charge—usually 8 percent if the purchase is under $25,000, and a smaller percentage if the purchase involves more than $25,000. The investor has the choice of withdrawing dividends and capital gains as they accrue or reinvesting them by buying more fund shares. Some funds allow reinvestment of profits. This can be a distinct advantage to the investor because it means he can purchase additional shares without paying the acquisition charge. The one-time purchase plan works best for the investor whose income is sporadic, such as a

writer or actor, or for the investor who has a one-time windfall to invest.

2. *Periodic Investment Plan:* This plan, which should not be confused with the New York Stock Exchange Monthly Investment Plan, permits the investor to make regular monthly or quarterly purchases in a mutual fund over an indefinite period of time. The minimum investment required usually is $50 a quarter. Most funds seek a commitment that the investor will participate in the plan for at least one year. The investor usually can vary the amount he pays into the fund, so long as it exceeds the minimum agreed amount. He also has the right to reinvest his earnings automatically.

3. *Contractual Investment Plan:* Under this plan, the investor signs a contract for a specified investment plan. These plans usually are written for certain periods of time, from one to twenty years, or for specified amounts, such as $10,000. One typical plan requires payment of $100 each quarter for ten years. Another calls for payments of $50 a month until $10,000 has been paid in. There usually is no penalty for missing payments, but if the investor fails to make payments for a period of one year the fund usually has the right to terminate the plan.

In the past few years, controversy has swirled around the practice of charging a "front-end loading" fee for contractual investment plans. By this practice, much of the total sales charge is collected in the first year of the plan. For example, in the case of the $50-a-month, $10,000 plan mentioned earlier, more than half the first year's investment of $600 could be eaten up by sales charges. If the investor sticks with the plan to completion, the sales charges average about 8 percent—basically the same as other plans. But if he drops out in the early years, he will find that much of his investment has gone toward paying the salesman's commission and other fund expenses.

Some states, including California, have banned this front-end loading. Supporters of contractual investment plans reply to criticism by observing that no investor should undertake a systematic investment plan unless he intends to complete it.

With more than 500 mutual funds now actively promoting their wares, how do you decide which one to choose? The task may look difficult, but with a few inquiries and a little research you can come up with an answer.

You might start by asking a reputable broker or mutual fund dealer to compile a list of mutual funds that match your investment goals. At the same time, you can obtain financial statements and sales literature issued by these funds.

There is another approach: Study impartial reference materials available at most brokers' offices and public libraries. Among them is "Investment Companies," published annually by Arthur Wiesenberger & Company. This statistics-filled volume is considered the "bible" of the mutual fund business. Another handy reference work is "Johnson's Investment Company Charts." In addition to charts on the performance of most mutual funds, it contains sixteen plastic overlays you can place on any graph to compare a fund's progress with that of the Dow Jones Industrial Average and major "blue chip" stocks.

As you narrow your list of potential selections, you will want to make some hard comparisons about the past performances of the mutual funds you are considering.

If you are interested in growth, find out which mutual fund shares have risen the most in price. Compare, too, the methods of distributing capital gains. Were gains distributed in cash or in the form of additional shares?

If current income is your objective, you should determine whether the fund provided a consistently high dividend income in relation to the current cost of a share.

If your goal is stability, find out how the price of a share held up in the stock market declines of the 1960s and 1970s.

There are several other factors which can be considered before you reach a final decision on what mutual fund to select. They include:

Life insurance: Some funds offer low-cost life insurance protection to their systematic investors. This is one way of assuring that your financial objectives will be reached even if you die prematurely.

Withdrawal plans: You may want to determine which funds provide withdrawal options that allow you to get some of your money back for retirement or other special purposes.

Reinvestment privileges: If you are not concerned with current income, you probably would seek information on the ease and cost of reinvesting dividends.

Operating costs: You should compare the annual overhead and expenses of several funds. These usually are expressed as a percentage of the fund's total assets.

There are other forms of investment which are tailored specifically for producing retirement funds. They are the subject of the next chapter.

CHAPTER 5

Funds
for
Retirement

An investment in an annuity is designed to provide income for a certain number of years, or for life, after you retire. Some people confuse it with life insurance policies since insurance companies also sell annuity contracts. The difference between a life insurance policy and an annuity contract is this: A life insurance policy promises to pay your beneficiaries a certain sum at your death. An annuity contract promises to pay you income while you live.

Does an annuity make sense for your family?

Before answering that question, you might estimate the retirement income you can expect from other sources. This can include income from Social Security, savings, investments, and a company pension plan. Is the income from these sources enough? That depends on the standard of living you expect to maintain in retirement. As a rough guide, most experts say an adequate retirement income should be at least 50 to 60 percent of your final working salary.

If there is a gap between anticipated income and the amount you estimate you would need, then an annuity might be helpful in bridging the gap.

There are two basic types of annuities. One is called a fixed-dollar annuity, the other a variable annuity.

The fixed-dollar annuity provides for a predetermined, unchanging income. The money paid by contract holders is invested in bonds and mortgages with a guaranteed return.

Under the variable annuity, the money paid in is invested primarily in the stock market. The income received by the person who purchased the annuity varies with the investment results. The variable annuity is designed to provide a hedge against inflation since stock market values tend to rise with increases in the cost of living.

There are several ways you can purchase an annuity.

Some families, when they are ready to retire, convert other investments into cash and buy an annuity with a lump sum payment. They begin receiving income under the contract immediately. Others make annual installment payments in the years before retirement and start receiving the income immediately after the last payment is made.

If you prefer, you can purchase an annuity prior to the time you want to start receiving the income. This is known as the deferred annuity. The company issuing the contract usually will guarantee you a minimum return on your deposits.

If you buy a deferred annuity contract, but die before you begin receiving payments, your beneficiary usually receives the amount you put into it, or the cash value of the contract, whichever is greater.

When you purchase a contract, you have a choice of several ways in which annuity income may be taken. All life annuities guarantee that payments will be made as long as you live. The principal options are:

• *Straight life annuity:* You receive regular payments while you are living, but the payments end when you die, whether death occurs after one payment or hundreds. This option furnishes the largest amount of income per dollar of purchase money, and it usually is selected by the person who needs maximum income and either has no dependents or has taken care of them through other means.

• *Life annuity with installments certain:* Under this option, if you die within a specified period after you start receiving the income, usually ten or twenty years, your beneficiary receives the regular payments for the balance of the specified period. The longer the specified period, the smaller the regular income payments.

• *Installment refund annuity:* If you select this option, but die before you receive as much money as you paid in, the regular income payments are continued to your beneficiary until total payments equal that amount.

• *Cash refund annuity:* This is similar to the installment refund option, except that your beneficiary would receive the balance of the original investment in a single sum.

• *Joint and survivor annuity:* With this option, two people—such as husband and wife—receive the regular income payments, and these payments continue so long as one of them is living.

The option you select has a bearing on the cost of the annuity contract. For example, according to rates quoted by one major company, a sixty-five-year-old man who wanted his annuity contract to guarantee him $100 a month income for life would pay in about $13,400 under the straight life option, about $15,200 under the installment refund or cash refund option, or about $17,425 under the joint and survivor annuity option—assuming his wife also was sixty-five.

An annuity contract for a woman costs more than for a

man, because women generally live longer than men and therefore are likely to receive the income for a longer period. In contrast, women usually pay lower rates for life insurance policies, since at almost any age their chances of death are less than those for men.

Annuities offer a tax advantage that can be significant, especially to those in high income brackets. Interest credited to annuity cash values is not taxable as income until after you begin to receive your annuity income. Since this often is in retirement years, you can expect to be in a lower tax bracket.

Two other major advantages of fixed-dollar annuities are:

• *Freedom from investment worry:* You know precisely how much you will receive in annuity income each month or each year. You won't be depending on dividend checks, which can vary in size.

• *Protection against a depression:* The company issuing the annuity contract guarantees that you will receive the specified payments, regardless of whether a depression strikes.

Among the disadvantages is the fact that little, if any, of the money you put into an annuity can be left to heirs. Your investment earns a relatively low return, and there is little hedge against inflation.

In the past two decades, inflation has eroded the dollar's purchasing power at an average rate of more than 2 percent a year. And economists point to the likelihood that inflation will continue.

Concern over the alarming shrinkage in the dollar's purchasing power is one reason for the increasing popularity of the variable annuity, designed especially to counter the effects of inflation.

Although variable annuities are the subject of legal controversy—principally over whether the contracts should be subject to state or federal regulation—more and more insurance companies are offering them.

Unlike the standard annuity, the variable contract does not provide a fixed-dollar income and is not supported by fixed income investments like bonds and mortgages. Rather, a variable annuity is backed by investments in such securities as common stocks, and the contract holder's income is based on the results of those investments.

Here's how a typical variable annuity might work:

If you signed a contract several years before your retirement, you would make regular premium payments during your working years. For these payments you would be credited with "units," or shares. The exact number of units would depend on the prevailing unit value of the fund's assets, consisting of payments made by all participants in the plan.

When you retire, you would receive each month the current value of the units you hold. For example, if you were entitled to payments of ten units a month, and the unit value in four consecutive months was $10, $9.90, $10.10, and $10.20, your retirement income for those months would be $100, $99, $101, and $102.

Proponents of variable annuities often cite the experience of the nonprofit College Retirement Equities Fund to show how this approach helps offset the eroding effects of inflation. The fund, which has some 150,000 college teachers and administrators as members, was established in 1952 and has served as a model for other plans established since.

Participants in this fund have the option of putting up to 75 percent of their payments into a variable plan, with the rest going toward a fixed-dollar annuity. Although the unit value of the fund may fluctuate daily as the stock market goes up and down, the fund's managers once a year establish the unit payout rate for the coming year. This gives

The Boom in Private Pension Funds

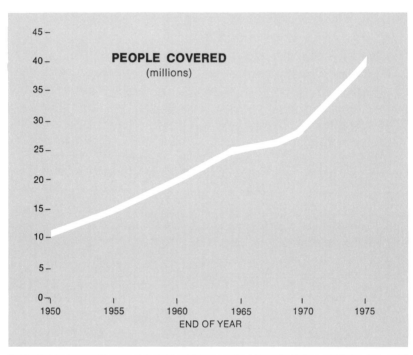

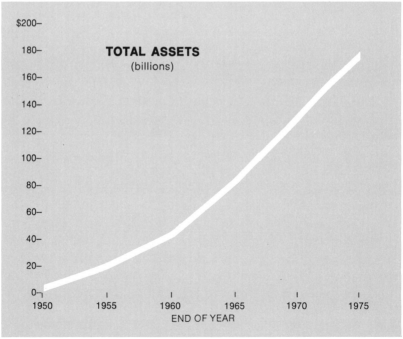

Sources: American Council of Life Insurance, SEC

participants more stability of income. Thus, participants did not feel the mid-1962 stock market drop until 1963, when the unit pay-out rate dropped from $26.13 to $22.68. But it climbed to $26.48 in 1964, $28.21 in 1965, and $30.43 in 1966. This means that a professor who retired in 1958, and received $265 the first year, was receiving more than $400 a month a decade later.

Corporate programs

During the past two decades, the growth of corporate retirement plans has been both rapid and widespread. One reason has been the tax advantage these retirement programs offer the employer. The money an employer places in a retirement plan is considered a business expense, and thus is tax deductible. Another reason has been the increasing competition for topflight employees and executives. Corporations have discovered that fringe benefits, including retirement plans, can be a powerful incentive for attracting and keeping personnel.

Corporate retirement programs vary widely. Under one typical plan, the company and the employee contribute equal shares into a fund. When the employee retires, money from the fund is used to purchase an annuity contract. This provides the retired employee with a monthly check. The size of the annuity contract usually depends on the employee's length of service and his average salary. In some instances, the company may bear the full expense of the retirement program.

Thousands of companies offer profit-sharing plans to their employees. Again, the plans differ from company to company. Under a typical arrangement, a percentage of the company's profits go into a fund—with each employee having a share in it. Some companies use a profit-sharing plan as the basis for a retirement program. Others offer a profit-sharing plan separate from a pension plan.

The Keogh plan

Corporate programs, of course, benefit corporate employees. What about the millions of Americans who are self-employed and thus do not have access to corporate retirement plans?

Some of the best tax news in years for the self-employed came when Congress passed the Employment Retirement Income Security Act of 1974. This modified a law passed earlier under the sponsorship of Congressman Eugene J. Keogh of New York. Thus these provisions of the tax law are commonly known as the Keogh Plan.

In brief, the law enables self-employed individuals to put aside retirement dollars and receive certain tax benefits. And it permits the nest egg to increase through compound interest or reinvested dividends, without incurring any tax liability during working years.

Here are more details on the act's basic provisions:

• Any sole proprietor or self-employed individual or partnership is eligible for the benefits of the act. This includes most professional people, such as doctors, dentists, lawyers, accountants, architects, writers, and artists, as well as owners of unincorporated business establishments, including retail stores, repair shops, and the like, and farmers. Ask yourself this question: Are federal income taxes withheld from your compensation? If not, then you probably fall into the self-employed category.

• You can set aside a maximum of 15 percent of up to $50,000 of your earned income for a Keogh fund plan. That is a maximum of $7,500 a year. You get tax breaks in two ways: the money you put into the fund is deductible from your income when you figure your income tax; and the money earned by the fund each year in interest or dividends is not subject to income tax at the time. When you retire and begin drawing money from the fund, you will have to pay tax, but by then you will presumably be in a lower income tax bracket since you will no longer be working.

• If you are a moonlighter, doing spare-time work as a consultant or similar practitioner, one provision of the act has special appeal. You can put all of the first $750 of your moonlighting income each year into a Keogh plan—the 15 percent rule does not apply until you have set aside $750.

Let's take an example of $1,000 put into a Keogh fund to see how the tax-saving provisions operate:

If your taxable income is $30,000 you would be in the 39 percent tax bracket. If you put $1,000 into a Keogh plan you would immediately save $390, since you could deduct that $1,000 from your $30,000 taxable income. If you earmarked the $1,000 for regular savings you would have only $610 left to put aside after paying the $390 in taxes.

Let's assume that you can earn 8 percent return on the money. After a year your $1,000 in the Keogh plan would have increased to $1,080. Your $610 in the regular, non-Keogh plan investment would have increased to $658.80, but you would have to pay $19.03 taxes on that gain, so you would be left with only $639.77. At this point your regular, non-Keogh plan investment is worth about 59 percent of your Keogh investment. And the margin becomes greater. During the seventh year the value of your Keogh investment would be worth double your regular investment. After ten years your Keogh money would total $2,158.92 compared with just $982.33 for your other money.

If each year you put $1,000 into your Keogh plan, the total fund after ten years would be worth $15,645.47. But if you took that same $1,000 each year, paid taxes on it, and put the remainder into a regular investment at the assumed 8 percent return, you would have a nest egg of just $8,002.01.

There are, of course, many details that apply to the program. For example:

• If you are self-employed but have other persons working for you, it may be necessary to set up pension plans for them in order to take advantage of a Keogh plan yourself.

• You will be penalized if you take money out of the plan before you are 59½ years old, unless you are totally disabled.

• You must take money out of the plan when you reach age 70½, even if you have not retired and still have current income.

Many banks, insurance companies, mutual funds, and other savings institutions have developed master plans that simplify the setting up of a Keogh fund. If an individual agrees to abide by all the provisions of an approved master plan, he can tie in with such a plan without filling out any forms for the Internal Revenue Service.

A similar program, known as Individual Retirement Accounts or IRAs, permits wage earners whose companies do not have retirement plans to set aside up to $1,500 a year for retirement with tax-shelter benefits similar to Keogh plans.

We have surveyed the task of planning an investment program and building an estate. But suppose you die before you complete your plan for family security? Life insurance can create an instant estate for you. It is the subject of the next section.

CHAPTER 6

The Role
of
Life
Insurance

Like millions of others, Joe Smith works for his earnings week after week, month after month, year after year. And Joe works hard, for two reasons. First, he wants to acquire wealth—not to become the richest man in the world, but to become financially independent, to be free of money worries. Second, Joe wants to leave an estate—a fair amount of capital which will provide for his family should he die.

With patience, perseverance, and planning, Joe can set aside a portion of his regular earnings, and then put the money to work through investments. In time Joe will acquire some wealth. And with proper planning, he can make certain that this wealth will pass on to his family.

But what happens if Joe dies before he has time to achieve his financial goals? Will there be an adequate estate for his family? Will there be enough to feed and clothe his wife and children? To keep a sound roof over their heads? To give his children a college education? To provide his wife with the peace of mind that financial independence provides?

What Joe needs is time to carry out his financial plans for building an estate of adequate capital. If fate should deny him that time, life insurance can step in to provide the resources he had not been able to raise himself.

It is said that life insurance buys time. It does so in the sense that it replaces some or all of the funds a breadwinner would have amassed had death not denied him the necessary time. Life insurance bridges the gap between what you have managed to build and what your dependents would need if you suddenly died.

In addition to serving this vital function, many companies have added investment features to their life insurance policies by offering cash values, retirement benefits, and college funds. This has created some confusion and argument over the two distinct roles served by policies—insurance against death and savings to be available in event of continued life.

These will be taken up later. Here we might emphasize the point that the basic job of life insurance is to provide protection against death in the interest of a surviving family rather than to provide funds to be enjoyed by the insured party and his family in later life. This function, served by what is commonly called "life" insurance, is sometimes more accurately described as "death" insurance.

Mention of insurance immediately raises a number of questions. How much do you need? What kind should you buy? From whom? In searching for the answers to these and other important questions, an individual and members of a family would profit by gaining some knowledge of the fundamentals of insurance, the different kinds available, how premium payments are calculated, how to secure information about and to choose between the more than 1,800

Over $2 Trillion in
Life Insurance Protection
Insurance in Force in the U.S.

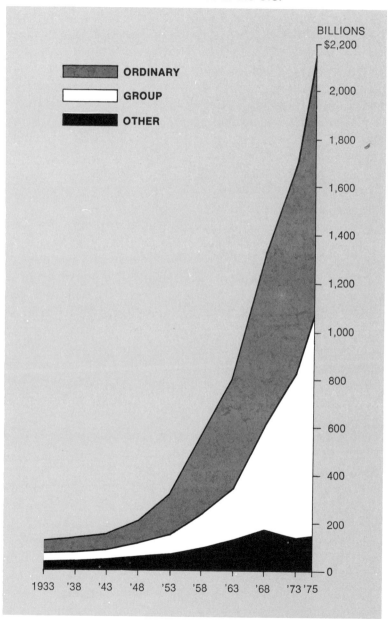

Source: American Council of Life Insurance

life insurance companies now operating in the United States.

While insurance is a highly technical subject, the basic concept is simple. Life insurance is a risk-sharing plan. A person joins a risk-sharing group (an insurance company) by buying a contract (a policy). Under the policy, the company promises to pay at the time of the policyholder's death a specified sum of money to the person or persons selected by him (the beneficiaries). In turn, the policyholder agrees to pay periodically a sum of money (the premium) to the insurance company.

The birth of insurance

Some historians trace the concept of insurance to the early Chinese and Babylonian civilizations, but the first recorded life insurance policy was written in a tavern in England in June 1536. Men who were in the business of insuring ships and their cargoes against the perils of storms and pirates gathered regularly in London's Old Drury Ale House. On that day more than four centuries ago, one marine underwriter, Richard Martin, proposed to his colleagues that they insure the life of William Gybbons, a "citizen and salter of London." For a premium of about $80, they promised they would pay Gybbons' family $2,000 if he died within one year. Gybbons accepted. As fate would have it, he died on May 29, 1537.

This first life insurance contract probably would have faded into history unnoticed had Martin and his associates simply paid the claim. But they balked, contending that the policy had been written in terms of lunar months of twenty-eight days each and had expired on May 20—nine days before Gybbons died. But Gybbons's heirs took the case to court, and the court ordered the claim paid, ruling that it was the underwriter's fault that the policy was unclear on what constituted a year.

For more than a century, life insurance remained little more than an occasional sideline for marine underwriters.

In 1692, the "Society for the Equitable Assurance of Lives and Survivorship" issued the first policies covering a person for his lifetime. Besides offering whole life insurance, the company introduced practices still standard in the industry. Level premiums graded according to age, a thirty-day grace period, a ninety-day reinstatement period, and a refund of premium overcharges set the pattern for the "dividend" payments of today. "Old Equitable," as it became known, today remains one of the strongest insurance companies in England.

The growth of life insurance in colonial America was slow. Benjamin Franklin is reported to have said: "It is a strange anomaly that men should be careful to insure their houses, their ships, their merchandise, and yet neglect to insure their lives, surely the most important of all to their families and more subject to loss."

The first corporation in North America to insure lives, the Presbyterian Minister's Fund, was founded in Philadelphia in 1759 and continues to operate today. By 1800, only 160 life insurance policies were in force in the United States. It was not until after the Civil War that the life insurance industry flourished in the United States. But with prosperity came chicanery, manipulation, and the squandering of funds. In 1905-1906, the Armstrong Committee of the New York Legislature issued a report which led to a New York Insurance Code and set the pattern for state regulation across the nation.

World War I stimulated the growth of life insurance. The government's war risk insurance introduced millions of soldiers to life insurance for the first time. The life insurance business ebbed during the Great Depression of the 1930s, but spurted during World War II when the government again offered low-cost life insurance to soldiers, while urging the civilian populace to purchase life insurance policies to combat inflation.

The volume of life insurance sales since World War II

has been little short of spectacular. In 1945, life insurance with a face value of about $150 billion was owned by Americans. Three decades later, this amount had increased to about $2 trillion. If this total were divided equally among all U.S. families, each would have $28,100 worth of life insurance. Seven out of ten Americans own life insurance. The average ownership for insured families is $33,100.

Getting to know companies and agents

The number of life insurance companies operating in the United States has tripled in the past twenty years. There are two basic types, stock companies and mutual companies.

A stock company, as the name implies, is owned by stockholders. They finance its operations and assume the risks and responsibilities of ownership and management.

A mutual company has no stockholders. It is owned by the policyholders. They elect a board which, in turn, directs the management of the company.

Working for these companies are about 500,000 insurance agents. How do you select a reputable one to handle your family's insurance needs?

Money management experts suggest you start by using the word-of-mouth approach. Ask trusted acquaintances to recommend an agent. Your banker and attorney can help in the search. Since life insurance may involve thousands of dollars in premiums over the years, the man you pick as your insurance counselor should be recognized by men in the financial field as someone who really knows money matters. Poor insurance advice, besides costing you a lot of money, could cause your family additional grief after your death.

A good life insurance agent keeps in touch with his policyholders. His advice and services are available at all times, even years after the initial sale. This is important, because from time to time you may have some big insurance decisions to make: Should you increase or decrease your coverage as your income fluctuates? Should you borrow against your policy's cash value? Should you revise your over-all insurance program when the children are grown? Should you change beneficiaries?

A life insurance agent either works directly for the insurance company or for an agency which may represent several companies. Either way, he receives commissions on premiums paid for the total amount of life insurance he sells. These commissions vary from policy to policy and company to company. On a typical permanent policy, the agent's first year commission usually ranges from 40 to 55 percent of the first year premium. For the next nine years, the agent generally receives about 5 percent of the annual premium as a commission. For example, if you bought a $10,000 permanent policy at an annual premium of $200, the agent would receive about $100 as his first year commission and about $10 a year for each of the next nine years.

In all states, an agent must secure a license from the state insurance commission or another regulatory board before he can sell life insurance. In many states, he must pass a written examination to qualify for a license. A good agent will have had extensive training. You may be more confident if he has earned the Chartered Life Underwriter (C.L.U.) designation. This means he has completed a rigorous set of college-level courses and has met other high professional standards.

You may want to consider picking an agent who is about your own age, or slightly older. He presumably has had insurance needs much like your own, and should understand your needs.

Be wary of an agent who urges you to drop an existing policy in favor of one he is selling. This practice can be costly. Here's why: If you drop an existing policy and take out a new one, you will have to pay again the company's initial administrative costs, including the salesman's commission. Also, if your present policy is several years old, the premiums for it probably are cheaper than they would be for a new policy. If your life insurance needs change, your existing policies usually can be adapted to meet your new circumstances.

As a general rule, experts advise against buying life insurance policies through the mail. One reason is that there is no personal counseling, as there is when you purchase insurance from an agent. Another is that the company offering insurance-by-mail may not be licensed in your state. If you are in doubt about the company's mail offer, consult your state insurance department or a local agency such as the Better Business Bureau.

Before seeking out an agent, or before one seeks you out, you might make yourself as knowledgeable as possible about life insurance. You could then conduct a more intelligent discussion and better evaluate the accuracy of an agent's statements. There are several good sources of information about life insurance:

1. *Your state insurance department.* In every state capital there is an insurance department, board, or commission ready to give you information about life insurance. This agency is available, too, should you have a complaint about an insurance company or insurance agent. In the event of disputes, the agency will see to it that you receive the protection of the state insurance laws.

2. *Your local Life Underwriters Association.* In most cities, there is a Life Underwriters Association composed of life insurance agents. These local associations are members of the National Association of Life Underwriters, with head offices in Washington, D.C. They will furnish information and assistance on life insurance matters.

3. *American Council of Life Insurance.* The council, an organization of life insurance companies doing business in the United States, serves as a central source of information about life insurance. It publishes a number of pamphlets

and booklets on life insurance, such as "Your Life Insurance and How It Works," "What's In Your Life Insurance Policy?", and "How Much Life Insurance Is Enough?" Single copies of these and other publications are free and can be obtained by writing the council at 277 Park Avenue, New York, New York 10017.

How your premiums are calculated

The insurance agent completes his explanations of the policy he's trying to sell. The customer asks his first question: "How much is the premium?" The agent thumbs through his little black book and, in a few seconds, has the answer.

The premiums listed in that little black book are based on years of scientific calculation. The key to the premium is a mathematical chart known as the mortality table. It is prepared by skilled insurance company employees, called actuaries, who study the proportion of people who die at various ages.

The most commonly used chart, known as the commissioners Standard Ordinary Table of Mortality, starts with ten million cases at birth. It follows them through age ninety-nine. For each year it shows how many of the original ten million will be living and how many will die, and gives the death rate per thousand at that age.

Suppose 1,000,000 children were born in the United States today. According to the mortality table, 966,499 of these would be living at age twenty. By age forty, there would be 924,136 still alive. By age sixty, the original group of 1,000,000 would number 769,870. By age eighty, the number living would have shrunk to 262,637. And by age ninety-nine, according to the table, 642 would be alive.

To illustrate how the mortality table is used in calculating premiums, let's suppose 10,000 persons age twenty joined together to form their own life insurance company. They each agreed to pay annually a sum sufficient to furnish

What Life Insurance Costs

Typical Annual Premium Rates Per $1,000 Policy

AGE AT PURCHASE	TERM (5-year Renewable and Convertible)	WHOLE LIFE	LIMITED PAYMENT LIFE (paid up in 20 years)	ENDOWMENT (20 years)
20	$ 8.30	$15.00	$23.80	$47.05
25	8.35	16.80	26.15	47.20
30	8.70	19.10	28.95	47.50
35	9.80	22.05	32.25	48.10
40	11.50	26.00	36.15	49.20
45	14.10	31.00	40.85	51.10
50	18.95	37.05	46.55	54.00
55	25.05	45.00	54.40	58.35
60	37.05	56.15	62.70	65.30
65	50.75	71.10	74.80	75.30

Note: Non-participating policies, level premium.
Source: American Council of Life Insurance

a $1,000 death benefit to families of those in the group who died during the year. According to the mortality table, eighteen of every 10,000 persons age twenty will die before reaching age twenty-one. In the first year, each of the 10,000 persons in the group would pay $1.80 to supply the $18,000 needed to pay the $1,000 to the families of the eighteen who would die.

If the same group, now numbering 9,982, wanted to continue the death benefit program for the next year, each would have to pay a little more for two reasons. First, there would be fewer individuals making contributions. Next, more of them would die during the year. By age sixty, only 7,966 of the original 10,000 persons in the group would be living. Before reaching age sixty-one, another 162 would die. To pay the $1,000 death benefit to the estates of the 162 who die would require $162,000—or $20.34 for each of the 7,966 who were alive at age sixty.

Under this year-by-year approach, the premiums increase each year. Most people prefer to pay the same amount in premiums year after year. Calculating the rates of "level" premium policies is a bit more complicated. Let's use the group of 10,000 persons age twenty to show how it is done. There will be 10,000 premiums paid by members of the group during the first year, plus 9,982 the second year, and so on. According to the mortality table, 508,703 annual payments would be made by members of the group before the last member died. Eventually the group must pay out $10 million in benefits. With 508,703 premium payments coming in, a premium level of $19.66 would produce that $10 million.

The group would collect more than enough money during the early years to meet the first claims. The extra amount would be available for investment. Assuming the company could earn interest on the investment of these funds, the interest could be used to help pay claims, reducing what policyholders would otherwise have to pay.

If the company earned just 3 percent interest, each member of the group would pay a premium of $9.56 a year instead of $19.66. The other $10.10 a year would come from the interest earned. Over the years, the policyholders would pay only $4,863,201 to insure benefits of $10 million.

These illustrations do not take into account a company's operating expenses nor the funds usually set aside to guard against investment losses, fluctuations in the death rate, and other contingencies. But they explain the principle. They show the factors taken into account by the insurance company when it calculates your premium.

Comparing the costs of insurance

The price of insurance, like that of other products and services, varies from company to company and policy to policy. In comparing the premiums on policies written by different companies, there are several points you should keep in mind. All life insurance policies fall into one of two categories—participating and nonparticipating or, as they are sometimes called, par and nonpar policies.

A participating policy pays dividends. These are not dividends in the sense of profits paid on stock, but refunds of the unused portion of premiums you have paid. A company which sells a participating policy sets the premiums at a rate higher than normally would be necessary. At the end of the year, after the company adds up the money it has paid out for death claims, operating expenses, and other requirements, it returns the excess money to policyholders as dividends.

A nonparticipating policy does not pay dividends. The company sets the premium rate at exactly the amount needed to cover anticipated costs of insurance coverage, company expenses, and profits. Nonparticipating policies usually are associated with stock companies, and participating policies with mutual companies. But some mutual companies sell nonparticipating policies, and some stock companies offer participating policies. In recent years participating policies accounted for 62 percent of all life insurance in force with American companies. The rest was nonparticipating.

When you compare prices, keep in mind that in the case of nonparticipating policies the premium rate is guaranteed in advance, while in the case of participating policies the actual cost to you is the premium less any dividends. The premium quoted for a participating policy is often higher than that of a comparable nonparticipating policy. But with the participating policy you are virtually assured of getting some of your money back in dividends. These dividends generally are not guaranteed and can only be estimated in advance.

It is impossible to know in advance exactly what the actual annual cost of a participating policy will be. But here's one way you can get an idea of the probable annual cost of a participating policy: Obtain from the insurance company figures on the average annual dividend it has paid in each of the past five years. Subtract the average annual dividend from the annual premium and you will have the probable —although not guaranteed—annual cost to you.

When you compare one policy with another, keep in mind that policy provisions may not be the same, even though the face value is identical. Some policies contain clauses that will be missing in others. The inclusion—or exclusion —of these clauses affects the prices of the policies.

It is easy to calculate the probable annual cost of a policy. It is the premium paid, less any dividends. It is more difficult to calculate the true long-term "net" cost. Insurance companies usually illustrate the long-term net cost by using a twenty-year projection. They add up the premiums due over the twenty-year period, subtract the anticipated dividends and the cash or surrender value after twenty years. This gives, they say, the policy's twenty-year net cost.

You save money when you pay your life insurance premiums on an annual basis. This is why: Insurance companies figure their rates on the basis of annual payments. If you pay on a semi-annual, quarterly, or monthly basis, the companies must do more bookkeeping, and they don't have use of your money for as long a time. For this reason, most insurance companies add a charge, sometimes 10 percent or more, if you make payments twice, four times, or twelve times a year. Thus, if the annual premium is $100, you could pay a total of $110 or more for the same coverage if you made your premium payments monthly.

But it is often difficult for families receiving their paychecks weekly or monthly to pay a large annual premium in one chunk. Here are some tips on how to stagger the premium payments and yet avoid the extra charges:

You can take out several small policies, instead of one large one, and have each payable in a different month.

Some companies offer what they call a premium deposit fund. This allows you to send the company varying amounts at irregular times in preparation for the next premium. If, for example, your next annual premium is $400, you could send in $25 one month, $75 another month, and so on. The company pays you interest on the money in the fund. Whenever the premium is due, it withdraws the right amount—$400 in this case—from your premium deposit fund. You can accomplish the same thing yourself by setting aside, either regularly or irregularly, enough money to cover the total premium when it comes due.

If you miss paying a premium on the date it is due, you have a grace period, usually thirty-one days, between the due date and the date the policy can be canceled for nonpayment. Some policies contain a provision that a loan automatically will be made against a policy's cash value to pay the premium and keep the coverage from lapsing.

We might next consider the different kinds of insurance available and the type which may best serve your needs.

CHAPTER 7

Choosing a Policy

There are three basic types of life insurance policies—term, whole life, and endowment policies. It is by combining the elements of these three basic types that the nation's insurance companies are able to offer thousands of seemingly different life insurance plans.

The main difference between the three types is this: Term policies simply offer protection against financial disruption that would follow the death of a family's breadwinner. Whole life and endowment policies combine this protection with features that allow you to accumulate cash savings while you are paying premiums.

The premium rates for the three basic types vary widely, mainly because of differences in the "savings" feature. Term policies do not acquire any cash value during your lifetime, and therefore cost less. Whole life policies cost more because they accumulate a cash value. Endowment policies are the most expensive because they essentially are savings vehicles. They pile up larger cash values in a shorter period of time.

Cash values are considered savings: They cannot be taken in full unless you surrender the policy. But you can borrow against the cash value, at interest, without giving up the policy. The interest rate usually is lower than that available at banks and other lending institutions.

When you buy whole life or endowment policies, a portion of your premium automatically goes toward building the cash value. This, in effect, is a forced savings plan. It might be especially attractive to those who have difficulty in regularly saving a portion of their earnings.

Let's examine the three basic types of insurance more closely and see how they can be used in your family security plan.

Term insurance

When you take out term insurance, you buy only insurance protection and nothing else. Fire insurance on your home is written on a term basis. If you buy a policy from a fire insurance company, you know you will collect nothing from the company unless your home is damaged or destroyed by fire. Your policy has no value when it expires.

Term life insurance works the same way. When you purchase term life insurance, you know that if you die within the period of time—or term—for which you are insured, the company will pay the beneficiary the face value of the policy. But if you are living when the term expires, the policy has no value.

Term life insurance policies usually are written for periods of one, five, ten, fifteen, or twenty years. Or, in some instances, they are written to expire at a certain age, such as sixty or sixty-five. Some term policies have "renewal" clauses. This gives you the right to renew the policy for

U.S. Families Are Buying
More Life Insurance

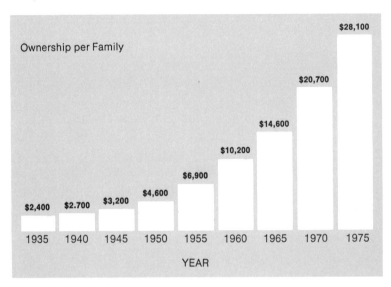

Source: American Council of Life Insurance

another term without proving you are insurable—in other words, without taking a medical examination. Another provision found in many term policies is the "convertible clause." This allows you to convert your term policy to a permanent policy, such as whole life, without a medical examination.

Including these two clauses in a term insurance policy will increase the premiums slightly, but insurance advisors say it usually is worth the money. There may come a time when you are unable to pass the insurance company's medical examination. But if these two clauses are included in the policy, you secure the right to renew your term insurance or convert it to permanent insurance without medical examination.

A few figures indicate the relative cost of term insurance. These, and subsequent figures, are simply representative examples. Actual premiums vary from company to company. A man aged twenty-five can buy a $10,000 five-year nonparticipating term policy, with renewal and convertible clauses, for about $83.50 a year. A $10,000 whole life policy would cost him about $168 a year—more than twice as much. However, at the end of five years the term policy would expire without value while the whole life policy already would have accumulated some cash value.

Another point about premiums for term insurance: The older the policyholder, the higher the premiums. The $10,000 five-year term policy which costs a man of twenty-five about $83.50 a year would cost him $87 a year if he renewed it at age thirty, about $98 a year if he renewed it at age thirty-five, and about $115 a year if he renewed it at age forty. At age fifty-five, the premium would be more than $250. If a man aged sixty-five sought a $10,000 five-year term policy, the cost would be more than $500 a year. By comparison, the premium on the $10,000 whole life policy cited earlier remains the same—$168 a year—for the man who buys the policy at age twenty-five and keeps it the rest of his life.

These figures show that term insurance, at younger ages, provides the largest amount of protection for the lowest cash outlay. For this reason, term policies often are purchased by young married men with small earnings but large insurance needs because their families are growing.

Here is an illustration:

Richard Williams, aged thirty, is a dentist who has just set up his practice. He and his wife have three children. He is in debt for his dental education and for equipment he bought to start his practice. He knows that in five years he will have these debts paid. He knows, too, that his income will increase steadily during those five years as he treats more and more patients and establishes his practice. To meet his insurance needs during this five-year period, he buys a $10,000 five-year term policy with renewal and convertible clauses. It costs him about $87 a year, about half what a $10,000 whole life policy would cost. At the end of the five years, he intends to convert the term policy to a whole life policy. He will be able to afford the difference in premiums then.

Two common uses of term policies are mortgage insurance and credit insurance. Mortgage insurance is designed to pay off the balance of a home mortgage if the policyholder dies. The principle of credit insurance is the same, but it covers personal debts instead of home mortgage. In both mortgage and credit insurance, decreasing term policies usually are issued. Coverage begins at one sum and gradually decreases as the balance of the mortgage or debt decreases. For example, if you purchased a $20,000 twenty-year mortgage policy, the death benefits would be about $10,000 at the end of the tenth year, the halfway mark.

Whole life insurance

Whole life is the most popular type of life insurance. As its name implies, it provides lifetime protection for lifetime payment of premiums. Whole life policies sometimes are known as straight life or ordinary life policies, and some insurance companies apply their own trade names to whole life policies. Slightly more than one-half of all life insurance now in force in the United States is classified as whole life. Term, endowment and combination policies make up the other half. The reason for the popularity of whole life policies is their flexibility. They combine protection with savings features and can be adapted to meet many different needs and family situations.

The premium rate for whole life insurance, while higher than for term insurance, is lower than for any other type of permanent insurance. Usually, the premium stays the same each year, even as you grow older. Like term insurance, a whole life policy pays the face value in death benefits. But unlike term insurance, it has what the insurance industry likes to call "living" benefits. You can borrow against its cash values, while maintaining the death protection benefits. If there is a loan outstanding at the time of death, however, the balance of the loan will be subtracted from the face value of the policy.

The cash value of a whole life policy is relatively small during the first few years because the insurance company must recover the cost of putting the policy into effect. But the value increases steadily in later years. For example, under one typical $1,000 whole life policy purchased by a man of twenty, the cash value would be only about $40 when he reached age twenty-five. But by the time he was forty years old, the cash value would be about $250, or one-fourth of the policy's face value. When he reached age sixty-five, the cash value would be $625—nearly two-thirds of the $1,000 face value.

Some whole life policies contain a special clause called the automatic premium loan. Under this provision, the company will automatically pay any premium that is not paid when due, charging such premium payments as loans against the cash value of your policy. This can be continued until the total of the automatic loans equals the cash value. Then the policy is terminated without further value.

If you own a whole life policy and you decide, say upon retirement, that you want to stop paying premiums, you usually can select one of four options:

1. You can cancel the policy and receive your cash value in a lump sum.

2. You can cancel the policy and receive the cash value in monthly installments for a specified period, or smaller monthly installments guaranteed for life.

3. You can use your cash value to pay for a reduced amount of paid-up life insurance for the rest of your lifetime—that is, a reduced amount of coverage without payment of any more premiums.

4. You can use the cash value to pay for a full amount of

protection for a specified period. The larger the cash value, the longer you can continue full paid-up insurance.

One form of whole life insurance is limited payment life. Instead of paying premiums for as long as you live, as you do with a whole life policy, you pay premiums on a limited payment policy only for a specified number of years—ten, twenty, or thirty. Or you may pay premiums until you reach a certain age, such as sixty or sixty-five. In either event, you are insured for your lifetime. Since you pay premiums for only a limited number of years, the annual premium rate is higher than for whole life. But since the premiums for limited payment policies are larger, the cash value of the policy increases faster.

Take the case of a man forty-five years old who bought a $10,000 whole life policy. His annual premium would be about $310. After twenty years, at age sixty-five, he would have a guaranteed cash value of about $4,500. If the same man bought a twenty-year limited payment policy at forty-five, the premium would be about $408.50 a year—about $100 a year more than that for a whole life policy. But at age sixty-five, the limited payment policy would have a guaranteed cash value of about $7,500—substantially more than the whole life policy.

For young families with a tight budget, limited payment policies may not be the best insurance plan. While it is true that cash values increase faster under a limited payment policy, you get less financial protection for your premium dollar. For example, a man of twenty-five whose family budget allows $200 a year for insurance could buy with that amount a whole life policy with a face value of about $12,000 or a twenty-year limited payment life policy with a face value of about $7,500. On the other hand, with the limited payment policy this young man would pay premiums for only twenty years. After that, he would be insured for life without further cost.

Limited payment policies have appeal for some, such as

professional athletes and entertainers, whose income may
be high for a short span of years.

Here is an example:

Hank Jones, an All-American fullback in college, has just
signed a professional football contract. He is virtually certain of drawing a large salary for at least ten years, but
he knows that when his football career ends, his annual
income will probably drop. So he decides upon a ten-year
limited payment life insurance policy. He pays premiums
for the ten years when his income is highest, and he receives
insurance protection for the rest of his life.

Similar to whole life coverage is a type of life insurance
known as industrial insurance. It is so named because it
was started about a century ago during the industrial revo-
lution and was first sold mostly to factory or industrial
workers.

Industrial life insurance policies are issued for small
amounts, usually less than $1,000. The weekly premiums,
sometimes as small as 5 cents, 10 cents, or 25 cents, are collected at the policyholder's home by the insurance agent.
These policies usually build up small values after the first
few years. But a large portion of the premium goes to
cover the insurance company's high administrative costs—
high because the agent must visit the home, write receipts
for very small sums, enter amounts in his record books,
and often take a few extra minutes to chat with the family.
Due to these overhead costs, the owner of an industrial life
insurance policy gets less coverage for his premium dollar.

Industrial life insurance is most popular among persons
with limited incomes. Census figures indicate that 12 percent of the families in the United States earn less than
$5,000 a year. Industrial insurance, because of the small
weekly premiums, is the only type of life insurance many
of these families can afford.

The amount of industrial life insurance in force in the

United States has declined steadily for several years, and now totals about $40 billion. The number of policies has dropped, too, and now totals about seventy-five million. The average size of these policies is $500.

Endowment policies

An endowment policy is essentially a savings plan. This is how the typical endowment policy works: When the policy is written, you select the date—called the maturity date —on which you want to receive the cash savings—or endowment—you will accumulate. This usually is at a certain age, such as sixty-five, or at the end of a certain period of time, such as twenty or thirty years. If you die before the maturity date, your beneficiaries are paid the face value of the policy. If you are living at the maturity date, you personally receive the policy's face value—roughly the same amount as your accumulated cash savings. But once you have received the full face value on maturity, you no longer have insurance protection. The company has paid off under the contract, and the policy terminates.

Endowment policies are expensive. Their premiums are higher than for any other type of life insurance. For example, an endowment policy maturing in twenty years would cost a man of twenty-five about $47.20 a year for each $1,000—or $472 a year for a $10,000 twenty-year endowment. This same young man could purchase $28,000 worth of whole life insurance for about the same cost.

Since they are designed to provide a definite amount of money at a definite time, endowment policies usually are purchased to meet a specific goal—a college education for children, a retirement fund for an individual now in his forties.

Endowment policies may appeal to persons who find it difficult to set aside regularly a portion of their earnings as savings. Since the premiums become a part of the family budget, just like house payments, the endowment policy in effect becomes a type of semi-compulsory savings plan.

Here is an example:

John Edwards, aged forty-five, is the manager of a super-market. Despite his best intentions, he has been unable to save consistently part of his current earnings for use during his retirement years. So he decides to buy a $10,000 endowment policy maturing when he reaches sixty-five. The premiums are high—$511 a year—but they become part of the family budget. Since he prides himself on paying his bills, he makes his premium payments on time.

An endowment policy may have been the answer in this case, since the policyholder's children were grown and his need for insurance protection was less. But endowment policies may not be ideal for younger people, especially young couples with small children. These families need protection against the financial disruption that would result from the death of the breadwinner. They need money for housing, food, and clothing. The premium dollar spent on an endowment policy does not buy nearly the amount of pure insurance protection as would a dollar spent on other types of policies. For this reason, insurance counselors often stress that endowment policies should be purchased only after the family's basic insurance needs have been met.

Another form of the endowment is the retirement-income policy. It is basically a savings contract that ceases being an insurance policy once the cash value exceeds the face amount. At death, the face value or the cash value, whichever is greater, is paid to the beneficiary. If the policyholder is living at maturity, the retirement-income policy is paid in monthly installments, rather than in a lump sum.

One point often raised by insurance counselors: Suppose you have a $10,000 twenty-year endowment policy and you die in the nineteenth year. Your beneficiaries would receive $10,000 but about $9,500 of it would be money you had accumulated under the policy's savings feature. Much more whole life insurance could have been purchased with the same money spent for the endowment policy.

Which type policy should you buy?

Of the three basic types of insurance policies, which should you buy? If you ask three different insurance men that question, you may get three different answers. One might say, "Term insurance is best for you." Another might say, "I would advise you to obtain whole life policies." And a third might say, "I think an endowment policy best suits your needs." The answers vary, of course, depending on your personal situation. But they also vary because there are differences within the insurance industry over which type of policy is best.

Some insurance counselors champion a "buy term and invest the difference" philosophy. Here's how their plan would work:

A man would buy enough term insurance to meet his family's needs in the event of his death. Much of this would be decreasing term insurance.

Then he would calculate the difference in the amount of premiums he pays for the term insurance, and the amount of premiums he would be paying had he bought permanent insurance.

That difference would be placed in a savings or investment plan each time he pays his insurance premiums. This way he would be building his own cash values. In theory, this personal investment plan would earn a higher return than an insurance company would pay on the cash values accumulated under a permanent policy.

Eventually, the cash values accumulated under this personal plan would more than offset the steady decrease in the face value of the term policies.

As the man grew older and the premiums on the term policies got larger, he would convert some of his term insurance to a permanent policy just big enough to cover final expenses and provide an income for his wife. This conversion would stabilize his annual insurance outlay, since permanent policies are of the level premium variety.

As advocates of permanent insurance are quick to point out, this "buy term and invest the difference" theory will work only if the insured has enough discipline to invest the "difference" each time he pays his insurance premiums.

Too often, they say, a man starts such a plan and then finds other uses for the money he should be investing. Then he ends up without adequate insurance protection—and without the cash values he was supposed to be building on his own.

Companies that specialize in permanent policies—whole life and endowment—direct much of their sales efforts at the millions of persons who have difficulty in sticking with a systematic savings plan. Permanent policies, they say, offer a painless way for a person to accumulate cash values while at the same time buying insurance protection.

Which type policy should you buy—term or permanent? If you can't make up your mind, then you might compromise by selecting a combination policy—one that combines term and permanent protection.

Combination policies

There are many variations of the three basic types of life insurance. And the number of variations seems to increase steadily as insurance companies strive to devise policies that will catch the eye of the public.

One of the most popular combinations is the family income policy. This combines term insurance with whole life insurance and is designed to provide supplemental income to the family, should the breadwinner die prematurely, in the important and most expensive years when the children are growing up. A typical twenty-year family income policy provides that if the policyholder dies within twenty years after he takes out the policy, his beneficiary will receive $10 a month for each $1,000 of the policy during the balance of the twenty years. In addition, at death or at the end of the twentieth year, depending on the terms of the policy, the beneficiary receives the face value of the policy, either in a lump sum or in monthly installments.

This is how the family income policy works:

Jack Evans, twenty-eight, and his wife have two sons, ages three and one. To make sure his family is protected against financial hardship should he die, he buys a $10,000 twenty-year family income policy. If he dies in two years, his family receives $100 a month—$10 per month for each $1,000 of the policy—for the balance of the family protection period, in this case eighteen years. These installments are paid from the term insurance portion of the policy. In addition, the permanent portion of the policy provides for payment of $10,000 immediately upon death, or in some policies, at the end of the protection period.

If he outlives the family protection period he has only a $10,000 whole life policy. The term portion that would have financed the monthly payments is no longer in effect, but the premium usually is lower after the family protection period ends. Family income benefits sometimes can be obtained by adding a rider to a whole life policy already in force.

The family-maintenance policy is a variation of the family-income policy. The main difference is that the monthly payments continue for a full twenty-year period after the insured dies. For example, if a man who purchased a twenty-year family-maintenance policy in 1968 died in 1978 his family would receive monthly payments for twenty years, or until 1998. If this same man had purchased only a twenty-year family-income policy in 1968 and dies in 1978, his family would receive monthly payments for the balance of the twenty-year family protection period—in this case ten years, or until 1988.

Both the family-income and the family-maintenance policies are available in ten-year and fifteen-year plans, as well
as the twenty-year plan.

The family-plan policy—not to be confused with family-
income or family-maintenance policies—is another combination of term and whole life coverage. The family plan is
simply a package of the two types of insurance covering
all members of the family. A typical family plan policy
places $5,000 in whole life insurance on the father, $1,000
in term insurance on the wife to age sixty-five, and $1,000
in term insurance on each of the children until they reach
a certain age, usually eighteen, twenty-one, or twenty-five.
In addition, children born after the policy is purchased are
automatically covered when they become fifteen days old.

Those are the major combination life insurance policies.
There are many other special policies offered by various insurance companies. They include:

• *Modified life policies:* These policies start with low-
cost term insurance for a specified period of time, usually
three to five years, and then convert automatically to
whole-life protection with its higher premiums. This may
be the ideal arrangement for a newly married couple or a
young professional man whose budget for insurance can be
expected to increase within a few years.

• *Extra-protection policies:* These also combine term
and whole life insurance in "double," "triple," and even
"quadruple" protection policies. The double protection policy, for example, may be $1,000 of whole life insurance
with $1,000 in term insurance added on. Triple protection
adds $2,000 in term insurance to the basic $1,000 in whole
life; quadruple protection adds $3,000 in term insurance to
the $1,000 in whole life. The term insurance usually contin-
ues until age sixty or sixty-five and then expires leaving the
whole life portion of the policy in force. These policies give
less protection for the extra-premium dollar than the family

policies, but the extra protection continues for a longer time.

• *Preferred risk policies:* These are regular whole life policies issued at special low rates to persons who are in the best of health and in the safest of jobs. Usually, a large amount of insurance—$10,000 or more—must be purchased under the preferred risk plan. For those who can qualify, preferred risk policies offer whole life insurance at very favorable rates. If you think you might be eligible for a preferred risk policy, ask your insurance agent.

Group insurance

Many business firms, labor unions and other organizations offer group life insurance to their employees or members. This is one of the fastest growing forms of life insurance. About ninety-six million persons now have over $900 billion worth of life insurance purchased through 380,000 group plans—more than double the number of persons and coverage of a decade ago.

One reason for the increasing popularity of group life insurance is that it often is the lowest-priced protection available. It is cheaper because the insurance company's administrative costs are lower. One master policy covering a large number of persons—from as few as twenty-five to as many as several hundred thousand—is issued by the insurance company in a single sale. In addition, the employer or sponsoring organization handles most of the individual bookkeeping.

In some cases, the employer pays the full premium. In others, where the employee and employer share the costs, the employee contributes his portion of the premium through the payroll deduction plan. Then the employer pays the insurance company a single sum covering the premium for the whole group.

All members of the group usually pay the same premium per $1,000 of coverage, since the cost is figured on the median age of all those participating. Thus, the cost advantage is especially great for older persons in the group.

Another advantage is that no medical examination is required. In this way, some persons are able to buy life insurance who, because of poor health, would otherwise be unable to obtain it.

When he leaves his job, an employee with group life insurance usually can convert all or part of his group coverage to an individual permanent policy without a medical examination. Of course, this individual policy will cost more than the group coverage. In a majority of the larger group plans and in an increasing number of the small plans, an employee retains at least a portion of his group insurance protection when he retires. Group insurance usually is term insurance, which means it does not build up cash values.

Another type of group insurance, called group permanent, is growing in popularity. This costs more, but when you leave your job you automatically get permanent, paid-up protection in an amount proportionate to the contributions you and your employer have paid into the plan. Under most group permanent plans, you accumulate cash values against which you can borrow.

Under the typical group insurance plan, your coverage is equal to one or two years' earnings. In a few plans, you have the privilege of buying, at extra cost, supplemental units of coverage without taking a medical examination. More and more group policies are providing low-cost protection for dependents of participating members. Coverage of dependents, however, now totals only a mere fraction of the total coverage of all group plans.

Insurance for business

While group insurance provides for employees, it does not help the employer in case of the loss of key men on whom the successful operation of an enterprise often depends. This has given rise to policies which protect an individual employer or a corporation against this type of loss.

Ruling in a case involving a business firm's purchase of insurance policies of the life of key employees, a federal judge observed:

"The business that insures its buildings and machinery and automobiles from every possible hazard can hardly be expected to exercise less care in protecting itself against the loss of two of its most vital assets—managerial skills and experience."

Life insurance has four common applications in the business world:

1. To protect a company against financial loss in the event of the death of a key man.

2. To salvage the value of a sole proprietorship upon death of the owner.

3. In a partnership, to prevent liquidation of the business upon death of a partner and to preserve the value of his share.

4. In a closely held corporation, to allow surviving shareholders to keep control of the business when a shareholder dies.

Life policies on key men—a president, vice-president, plant superintendent, bookkeeper or foreman who would be difficult to replace—are held by the company. Proceeds from policies go to the company and can be used to offset any losses or extra expenditures. Cash values that build up in such policies are carried as assets, and the company can borrow against them.

The sole proprietorship—an unincorporated business owned by one man—is the most common type of business in the country. Small shops and stores can be found in every hamlet, village, town, and city. While the sole proprietorship is the simplest type of business to establish, it also can be one of the most dangerous. This is why: There is no legal distinction between the assets of the business and the assets of the owner. In the eyes of the law, they are one and the same.

Upon death of the owner, the assets of a sole proprietorship become part of the owner's general estate. This means all business debts, as personal debts, would have to be paid from the same estate. Unless the owner's will specifically provided for continued operation of the business, or unless his heirs agreed to take over the business, the executor of the estate would have to liquidate it. Liquidation means forced sale. Forced sale almost always means loss.

By purchasing a life insurance policy payable to his estate, the sole proprietor can make certain that his business debts would not drain the estate he leaves his family. At the same time, the policy would indemnify his heirs for the loss that usually results from a forced sale of a business. Meanwhile, the policy's cash values could serve as an emergency fund for the sole proprietor.

The death of a partner automatically dissolves a partnership. It becomes the duty of the surviving partner to wind up the affairs of the business without delay. He must collect all accounts and convert all assets into cash, turning over the deceased's share to his estate. If the debts of the partnership are greater than the assets, then the estates of both partners are liable. Frequently it becomes necessary to liquidate the business with a financial loss.

This problem can be avoided if the partners agree that, upon the death of one of them, his estate will sell and the surviving partner will buy his interest in the business. This buy-sell agreement can specify the purchase price, or the method of determining it. In this way, each partner is assured that his heirs will receive a fair price.

There remains, of course, the problem of how the survivor will raise the money to buy his late partner's share. Life insurance is one solution. Each partner buys and owns a policy on the life of the other. The death benefits are

What Insurance Companies Paid
On Policies

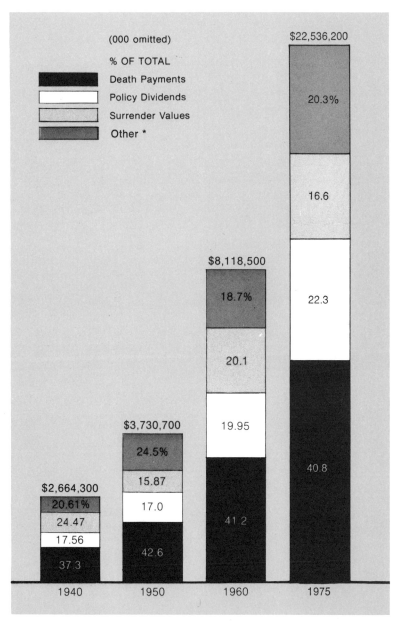

(000 omitted)

% OF TOTAL

■ Death Payments
□ Policy Dividends
▨ Surrender Values
▧ Other *

$22,536,200

20.3%

16.6

22.3

40.8

$8,118,500

18.7%

20.1

19.95

41.2

$3,730,700

24.5%

15.87

17.0

42.6

$2,664,300

20.61%

24.47

17.56

37.3

1940   1950   1960   1975

° Annuity payments, matured endowments, and disability payments

Source: American Council of Life Insurance

pledged to execute the buy-sell agreement. If there are more than two partners, it may be simpler for the firm to hold the policies on the life of each partner. The death benefits would go to the firm, which then would buy the deceased partner's interest from his estate.

The vast majority of corporations do not publicly offer their stock for sale. They are classified as "closed corporations" and, in effect, are little more than incorporated partnerships. The relationship among stockholders usually is as close as that among members of a partnership.

Unlike a partnership, a corporation's legal life does not automatically end with the death of a stockholder. The shares of stock go to his estate or his heirs. To keep control of the stock, a buy-sell agreement can be drafted while all stockholders are alive. This would pledge the estate of a deceased stockholder to sell the stock and the surviving stockholders to buy it. It also would fix the price, or determine the method of setting the price. The problem once more arises of how to finance the stock purchase. Again, life insurance is one answer. A policy on the life of each stockholder would make certain that money for the purchase would be there when needed.

It is best to seek the assistance of an attorney in drafting buy-sell agreements. The legal and taxation issues involved often are complex, and an attorney can help avoid many pitfalls.

There are other advantages of business life insurance. It can strengthen credit and provide collateral for business loans. Creditors of a business feel safer when they know that, should a key executive, sole proprietor, partner, or major stockholder die suddenly, life insurance guarantees that the business would remain in operation or would provide the money to offset losses. Most banks and other lending institutions readily accept cash values of life insurance policies as collateral for loans.

G.I. Insurance

During World War I, World War II, and the Korean War, the government offered low-cost life insurance—commonly called G.I. Insurance—to millions of men and women serving in the armed forces. Veterans who have not taken full advantage of the right to buy G.I. Insurance, or convert it to a permanent form of coverage, may want to contact their local Veterans Administration office for the latest information, since many experts rate these government policies as the best life insurance bargain available. The maximum allowable coverage is $10,000.

The insurance made available during World War I is known as United States Government Life Insurance (USGLI). It was issued as five-year term, whole life, limited payment life, and endowment policies. Veterans of World War I who hold USGLI term insurance can renew it for five-year periods or convert it to one of the permanent types of insurance.

Insurance issued by the government to members of the armed services during World War II and up until April 25, 1951, is known as National Service Life Insurance (NSLI). Originally, NSLI was sold only as five-year, level premium participating term insurance. It may still be renewed for five-year periods without a medical examination, or it can be converted into permanent whole life, limited payment, or endowment policies. The cost of NSLI was, and still is, very low for several reasons. The government decided not to use any premium funds to pay operating costs. Also, money appropriated by Congress, not premium funds, was used to pay benefits to families of men who died in service or later because of service-related disabilities. Casualties during the war were fewer than anticipated, and dividend payments since then have been generous.

Korean War veterans and others who served at least thirty-one days between June 25, 1950, and January 1, 1957, were covered under the Servicemen's Indemnity and Insurance Acts of 1951. They automatically had, free of charge, $10,000 in life insurance while on active duty. Upon leaving the service, they could apply for a level premium term policy that could be renewed every five years. Face value of the new policy could not exceed $10,000. In 1958, a law was passed allowing Korean War veterans to convert their term policies to a variety of permanent plans. This can be done without taking a medical examination.

Insurance for women

When a family sits down to discuss its life insurance needs, this question often arises: Should the wife have life insurance?

The answer usually is yes. Seventy percent of all women over eighteen in the United States do have life insurance. But many experts say that when it comes to life insurance, the opposite of the lifeboat rule should be applied. In other words, "Women and children last." These experts say that before a husband considers buying insurance on his wife's life, he should make certain he has adequate insurance protection of his own. If the husband is fully covered, he may want to examine the low-cost possibilities of covering his wife in a family plan policy or through a rider that can be attached to a policy he already owns.

Here's why it may be wise to have life insurance on a wife and mother:

A surviving husband left with children at home would find it expensive to hire an outsider to care for the youngsters, do the housework, and prepare the family's meals. While no one likes to place a monetary value on life, it should be recognized that a husband would lose the savings of joint-return income tax rates should his wife die. His disability and retirement benefits under Social Security would be less.

If a wife works outside the home—as one of every three does nowadays—and part of her salary goes toward paying the family's living expenses, her death could cause severe financial problems. This might be taken into account when insuring her life.

Unmarried women may need life insurance too. This is especially true of a career woman with dependents. She is her family's breadwinner, whether the dependents are children or elderly parents. Her life insurance needs likely would be similar to those of a family man.

A career woman without dependents may have less need for the financial protection afforded by life insurance. But she may want to use the savings features of life insurance policies to set aside funds for her retirement years. Some insurance companies sell short-term endowment policies designed for the single working girl planning marriage who wants to save for wedding expenses or to furnish her dream home.

One bright note here: Since the life expectancy of women is longer than that of men, life insurance rates for women usually are lower.

Insurance for children

Should policies be taken out on the lives of children? Insurance counselors say the family should make certain there first is adequate coverage of the family's breadwinner. Even when the breadwinner is adequately insured, they say it may not always be wise to buy insurance on a child's life.

A life insurance policy on a small child obviously would not pay off if the father died. Unless the widow could continue to pay the premiums, the child's policy would lapse. Some policies include a "payer benefit." Under this clause, further premiums on a child's policy are waived if the payer, usually the father, dies before the child is twenty-one.

Some families buy life insurance for children to cover medical and funeral expenses in the event a child dies. These final costs could range from a few hundred dollars to more than $1,000. Coverage in these amounts is available through family plan policies or through a rider attached to the father's policy.

Millions of parents are using the savings features of life insurance to set aside money for their children's college educations. If this is the case in your family, it might be wise to make sure the policy is in the name of a parent, instead of the child. Should the parent die, the money would become available without further premium payments. Educational policies can be expensive, since many of them are endowment plans. Some authorities argue that the money placed in such insurance policies could draw higher interest if invested elsewhere, such as a savings and loan association.

One heavily advertised special plan for children is known as the "jumping juvenile policy." It usually provides $1,000 in coverage to age twenty-one, when it automatically increases five-fold without an increase in premiums or a medical examination. The premium rate after age twenty-one is attractive. Before age twenty-one, it is expensive.

New trends in life insurance

The life insurance industry has steadily been losing its share of the public's savings dollar. Twenty-five years ago, about 50 percent of every dollar saved by Americans was invested in cash-value features of life insurance. Today the figure is less than 20 percent.

More and more savings have been going into deposits at commercial banks and into such investments as mutual funds. The attraction of mutual funds, of course, is the promise of a greater return on a given amount of invested capital than can be expected from life insurance. The force of inflation, eroding the purchasing power of the dollar, has been an important element in attracting people to seek greater gains through mutual funds. The purchasing power of the face value of a given life insurance policy has been falling continuously as a result of inflation over the years.

To counteract this trend, insurance companies have begun to combine the benefits of life insurance with the promises of mutual funds. This arrangement enables them to offer the public variable annuities which rise in value to offset increasing prices and the consequent fall in the dollar's purchasing power. Some experts anticipate a considerable development in this direction. The public is likely to be attracted to policies with cash values which, partly invested in common stocks, will rise as the value of stocks rise. The danger, of course, is that they could also fall should the price of stocks decrease.

8

How
Much
Coverage?

How much insurance should you carry?

It is one of the more difficult questions to answer. Everyone naturally wants as much protection as he possibly can secure for the future—for himself and for his family. In calculating the amount of insurance to be carried, one must strike a balance between what he would like in the future and what he can pay for insurance premiums at present.

In general, you go about finding the answer to the question by estimating the amount of assets you hold at the present time, and calculating the amount of money that will be necessary to meet the cost of your family's future needs. The difference between the two amounts, assuming there is a deficit—as is the case with the great majority of families—provides a rough indication of how much insurance you must carry to bridge the gap.

Some authorities suggest this rule of thumb: The breadwinner in the family should have life insurance with a face value three to five times his annual income.

But because no two families have exactly the same needs, using this formula could give you the wrong answer. Two examples illustrate this point:

Samuel Jones, age fifty-five, earns $75,000 a year as president of his own company. He and his wife inherited $100,000 a few years ago and have invested it wisely. They have no children living at home. Using the formula mentioned above would mean Mr. Jones should have $225,000 to $375,000 in life insurance. This is probably far more than needed since their investments likely would assure his wife an adequate income for the rest of her life.

John Adams is twenty-six and just started work at an $8,000-a-year job in a factory. He and his wife have three boys. Using the formula cited earlier, he should have between $24,000 and $40,000 in life insurance coverage. But should he die, this may not be enough to provide an adequate income for his family while the children are young, to say nothing of realizing his hopes that all three boys attend college.

Though there is no magic formula for determining how much life insurance you should carry, there are six basic points you should take into account when you think about a family security plan. They are:

1. *Cash for immediate needs:* This covers the increasingly high cost of dying—hospital and doctor bills, funeral expenses, estate settlement costs, and perhaps estate taxes as well as current bills and installment debts. Medical costs of a final illness or fatal accident could require $2,000 or more in cash.

2. *Readjustment fund:* When the breadwinner dies, families need time to consider carefully some important ques-

tions. Should they sell the house? Should they sell the family business? Should they move, especially if it means the children will have to change schools? Should the widow take a job? If so, does she need special training? Hasty decisions could prove costly. A readjustment fund, perhaps equal to six months or a year of the husband's income, could give a family time to make the right decisions.

3. *Family income:* This covers the cost of operating a household—food, housing, utilities, clothing, medical bills, school expenses—while the children are growing up. By one suggested guideline, a family needs about half the father's monthly income for this purpose. But other experts say that in this era of high living costs a widow with two children should figure on a minimum of $500 a month. Your estimates should cover the time until the youngest child has finished his schooling.

4. *Education:* You probably will need at least $1,500 a year to send each child to college, even with partial scholarships and part-time jobs. College costs across the country now average about $3,000 a year. At some colleges expenses run as high as $5,000 a year. And college costs are increasing every year.

5. *Emergency fund:* This would be a liquid cash reserve that could be tapped quickly to meet an unexpected crisis, such as a major illness. Depending on the size and health of your family, most counselors say $1,000 to $3,000 should be set aside in an emergency fund. This money, if invested properly, could be earning interest until needed.

6. *Income for the widow:* Once the children are on their own, the wife's need for income usually drops. If she has remarried or gone to work, she may need no income at all. But to be on the safe side, some authorities suggest that one-fourth of the husband's monthly earnings be figured as the amount of income needed by a widow after the children leave home. Other experts, citing the steady rise in the cost of living, say $350 a month should be the minimum amount.

With these six points in mind, you can by simple arith-metic calculate the approximate needs of your family should the breadwinner die prematurely.

Social Security

The Social Security identification card in your wallet means you may be eligible for thousands of dollars in bene-fits, and these should be taken into account in calculating the amount of insurance you should buy.

The basic idea of Social Security is simple: During work-ing years, employees, their employers, and self-employed people pay Social Security taxes into special funds. When earnings stop because the worker retires or dies, monthly cash benefits are paid from the special funds to replace part of the earnings the family has lost.

While the basic idea behind the system is simple, the method of computing benefits is not. In fact, it is so complex and involves so many charts and formulas that you would be wise to call or visit your local Social Security Administra-tion office for a detailed explanation and an analysis of your potential benefits.

Here, however, are some general guidelines to help you make rough calculations.

To be eligible for monthly retirement benefits, you must have credit for a certain amount of earnings you paid into the Social Security fund. Just how much credit you must have to be fully insured depends upon your date of birth and the year you reach retirement age—sixty-five if you are a man and sixty-two if you are a woman.

The government has been collecting Social Security taxes since 1937, and it has been paying out monthly benefits since 1940. The law was changed in 1951, and there is a difference between the method of calculating credits acquired before 1951 and the credits acquired since then.

If you reached retirement age in 1971, you will be fully

insured if you have credit for five years' work. If you reached retirement age in 1973, you will need five and one-half years of credit; in 1975, you will need six years' credit; in 1977, you will need six and one-half years' credit, and so on until 1991. If you reach retirement age in 1991 or thereafter, you will need ten years of credit.

If you die before you reach retirement age, you will be considered fully insured and your survivors would be eligible for monthly benefits provided you had credit for one and one-half years' work since 1951, omitting any years before you became twenty-two. If you become disabled before you are twenty-four, you need credit for one and one-half years of work in the three years before you become disabled. If you become disabled between twenty-four and thirty-one, you need Social Security credits for half the time after you are twenty-one and before you become disabled. To get disability benefits if you become disabled at thirty-one or later, you must be fully insured and have credit for five years of work in the ten years just before you become disabled.

Your average earnings covered by Social Security over a number of years determine the amount of benefits to which you and your family will be entitled. Again, complex formulas are used to determine your average earnings. For the sake of simplicity, consider the law since 1951:

List the amount of your annual earnings on which you have paid Social Security tax starting with 1951 or the year you became twenty-two, if later. The maximum earnings creditable for Social Security are $3,600 for 1951–54; $4,200 for 1955–58; $4,800 for 1959–65; $6,600 for 1966–67; $7,800 for 1968–1971; $9,000 in 1972; $10,800 in 1973; $13,200 in 1974; $14,100 in 1975; $15,300 in 1976; and $16,500 in 1977.

You are allowed to exclude five years of low earnings —or no earnings—from the list. Then add up the annual totals, and divide by the number of years listed. This gives you an approximate figure for your average yearly insured earnings. Then a glance at the table on page 175 will tell you what you can expect to receive in Social Security benefits.

Remember this: the Social Security Administration stands ready to help you determine how the complex formula applies in your particular case. Requests for information, for copies of records, or to inspect or copy records may be made at any of the 860 district and branch Social Security Administration offices. Similar requests relating to information and records available in the Bureau of Hearings and Appeals may be made at any of its sixty-three field offices.

The Social Security program currently is financed with a tax on the first $16,500 in annual earnings of each insured person. The amount paid in by the employee is matched by his employer. Self-employed persons pay at a rate of about one and one-half times the employee's rate. Included in the monthly contribution is a payment to help finance the hospital insurance portion of the Medicare program.

This table shows the combined Social Security and Medicare tax rate for the present and for years to come:

| | *Percent of Covered Earnings* | |
Year	*Employee/Employer (Each)*	*Self-Employed*
1974-77	5.85%	7.90%
1978-80	6.05	8.10
1981-85	6.30	8.35
1986-98	6.45	8.50
1999-2010	6.45	8.50
2011 & Later	7.45	8.50

Maximum Earnings Covered: $16,500

The Social Security laws passed by Congress in 1972 and 1973 provide for automatic increases in both Social Security benefits and covered wages to take account of increases in living costs and wages.

Keep in mind that the benefits, the tax, and other figures

cited are subject to revision in the years ahead. Congress periodically increases the monthly benefit payments. This usually is accompanied by a boost in the tax rate.

Remember, too, that benefits are not automatic. Before they can start, you or your survivors must file an application with your local Social Security Administration office.

How to figure your family's needs

Some simple arithmetic by the John Allen family illustrates how you can calculate the approximate needs of your family should the breadwinner die before his financial goals are achieved. John is thirty-five; his wife, Sue, is thirty-one. They have two children, age six and nine. John and Sue, pencil in hand, went through the list of six needs. Assuming John would die next week and that his wife would never remarry, here is what they found.

1. *Cash for Immediate Needs:* After reviewing their outstanding debts and their health insurance policies, they estimated the needed cash at $2,500.

2. *Readjustment Fund:* They figured this at half of John's $12,000 annual earnings, or $6,000.

3. *Family Income:* To be on the safe side, they estimated Sue would need $600 a month to meet household expenses during the sixteen years—192 months—until the youngest child was twenty-two. This totaled $115,200.

4. *Education:* Computing the cost of college at $3,000 a year for each child, they came up with a total of $24,000.

5. *Emergency Fund:* They decided the amount set aside for emergencies should be $2,000.

6. *Income for the Widow:* Once again to be on the safe side, they calculated Sue's income needs after the children left home at $400 a month. This need would begin when Sue was forty-seven, and assuming a life expectancy of seventy-four years, would total $129,600.

John and Sue added up their estimates. They were astounded by the total needs: $279,300.

"How," they wondered, "can we ever find a way to reach that goal?"

Before they became too discouraged, this family investigated to find out what resources would be available to help meet their needs. These included their own assets, Social Security and Veterans Administration benefits, and death benefits paid by some employers, some unions, and other associations.

First, the Allens took a look at their personal assets. They figured they had $10,000 equity in their home. Other assets consisted of a $4,000 savings account and $1,000 in government bonds, plus Mr. Allen's interest in a small business which they estimated was worth $25,000. Thus the Allens had $40,000 in assets. They subtracted this from their "needs" figure and came up with a new total: $239,300.

Some families take the widow's potential earning power into account. Because of uncertainties involved, many estate planners say a widow's potential earning power should be either left out or purposely underestimated. Mrs. Allen said she would return to work after the children left home. But Mr. Allen decided to underestimate her probable earnings, since the employment market for middle-aged women, excepting those with special training or skills, is limited. The Allens calculated Mrs. Allen could earn $200 a month from the time she was forty-seven, when the youngest child left home, until she would retire at age sixty-two. This totaled $36,000. Subtracting this from their revised "needs" list gave them a new total: $203,300.

Then the Allens examined the benefits their family would receive under Social Security.

First they found that Social Security pays a lump sum death benefit. This is equal to three times the amount of monthly retirement benefits at sixty-five, up to a maximum lump-sum payment of $255. In addition, families of all veterans are eligible for a $250 lump-sum death benefit.

Then they calculated the amount of Social Security survivor's benefits effective beginning June 1976. The maximum Social Security survivor's benefit ends when a child reaches eighteen unless he is still in school. Benefits continue for a child in school until the age of twenty-two. If the husband died, the Allen family would become eligible for the maximum Social Security benefit of $739.10 a month. For twelve years, until the younger child reached eighteen, the widow and children would receive monthly benefits totaling $106,430. For one more year, until the older child completed college, the children would receive $633.60 a month, a total of $7,603. For a further three years, until the younger child completed college, the monthly benefit would be $316.80, totaling $11,405. These Social Security benefits would supply $125,438 toward meeting the needs of the family until the younger child is twenty-two.

Mrs. Allen would then be forty-seven years old. She would not receive benefit payments again until she reached the age of sixty. Then she could file for full widow's benefits of $302 a month. A widow is eligible for payments even if she never held a job covered by Social Security. In effect, the benefits she receives are those which would have gone to her husband had he lived.

The Allens, calculating a life expectancy of seventy-four years for Mrs. Allen, figured she would receive a total of $50,736 in widow's benefits starting at age sixty.

This is how the Allens' Social Security benefits added up:

Death benefits	$ 255
Family income benefits	125,438
Widow's retirement	50,736
Total	$176,429

The Allens subtracted this amount from their revised "needs" list. Their new total: $26,871.

This, they saw, was the approximate amount that should

be covered by Mr. Allen's life insurance. They surveyed their present policies—$5,000 in GI Insurance, $5,000 in group coverage, and a $2,000 whole life policy, for total coverage of $12,000. This left a gap of $14,871. But the family did not necessarily need precisely that amount in additional insurance. A lesser sum, perhaps $10,000, could be sufficient, since assets in the estate would earn substantial interest over the years if handled properly.

Mortgage insurance

Millions of Americans call themselves home-owners. But in a great majority of cases the home carries a sizeable mortgage, almost always repayable in monthly installments. The death of the family's breadwinner does not end the obligation to make these payments, and selling the home under such trying conditions often is not a practical or possible solution. One answer is mortgage insurance. This special policy is designed for only one purpose: to pay off the mortgage upon death of the breadwinner.

These policies are sold under many different names, such as "mortgage protection," "mortgage redemption," and "home protector." Most are simply a form of level premium decreasing term insurance. The premium remains the same for the period of the mortgage—usually fifteen, twenty, twenty-five, or thirty years—but the amount of coverage decreases as the balance of the mortgage gets smaller. Actually, any kind of insurance policy that will provide a fund large enough to retire the balance of the mortgage would serve the purpose.

Some mortgage insurance policies specify that the proceeds will be paid in a lump sum to the beneficiary upon death of the policyholder. Other policies provide that the proceeds can be paid in monthly installments equal to the mortgage payments. The latter is useful if the mortgage terms do not allow prepayment.

Credit insurance

Credit life insurance is similar to mortgage insurance. It is designed to repay a personal debt should the borrower die before completing the payments. It was first introduced in 1917 and in recent years has become the fastest growing form of life insurance in the United States, keeping pace with the ever increasing rate of installment buying. There are now more than eighty million persons in the United States with credit life insurance coverage—double the number a decade ago. Total coverage has doubled in the same decade. It now stands at more than $100 billion. The average policy coverage is about $1,250. Despite its rapid growth, credit life insurance still accounts for less than 7 percent of all life insurance in force in the United States.

Credit life is term insurance, generally decreasing as the loan is repaid. More than four-fifths of such insurance is handled through 90,000 group plans now in effect. Insurance companies issue master credit life insurance contracts to banks, finance companies, credit unions, retailers, and other lenders. These lending agencies then simply extend the coverage to each individual borrower. Sometimes the borrower can decide whether he wants credit insurance, but many lenders make such coverage mandatory.

An example of how credit life insurance works:

John Jones borrowed $500 from his bank. In granting the loan, the bank extended its master credit life insurance policy to cover the borrower. The premium is included in his monthly payments. If Mr. Jones dies before he fully repays the loan, the insurance will pay the balance due at the time of his death, freeing his family from this indebtedness.

The cost of credit life insurance generally is modest. But authorities urge the consumer to remain alert. To avoid being overcharged, the borrower might ask to be shown the cost and coverage of insurance included in the sales contract or loan agreement he is negotiating.

Health insurance

Life insurance protects against loss of income due to death of a family's breadwinner. But it does not protect against two perils—illness and injury—that can rob a family of its future income, wreck its savings account, and leave it with staggering hospital and medical bills.

To cope with these financial uncertainties, you can purchase health insurance protection. The insurance industry reports more than three-fourths of the nation's civilian population has "some form of health insurance protection through voluntary insurance organizations . . ." But many experts believe that most families have inadequate health insurance, or the wrong kind. They point out that in recent years insurance has paid only about one-third of the public's medical bills.

Many employers and other organizations, such as labor unions and fraternal groups, offer group health insurance just as they offer group life insurance. Group policies generally are cheaper than individual policies because administrative costs are lower.

In brief, health insurance is designed to help pay hospital, doctor and other medical bills, and to help make up the income lost because of illness or injury. Only rarely will a health insurance policy pay the full costs incurred. But by picking up a big portion of the bills, the policy can take much of the financial pain out of illness or injury.

The basic types of protection offered by health insurance policies are:

1. *Hospitalization:* This pays all or part of the bill for room and board in the hospital, up to the number of days specified in the policy. In addition, charges for medicine, X-rays, anaesthesia, and the use of the operating room usually are covered up to maximum amounts, also specified in the policy.

2. *Surgical:* The policy specifies the maximum sums that

will be paid for surgery. In one typical policy, it ranges from $35 for a tonsillectomy to $300 for heart surgery.

3. *General Medical:* This covers specified nonsurgical expenses. The extent of coverage varies widely from policy to policy. For example, one policy may cover all charges for use of a hospital emergency room, while another may pay only a part, or even none, of the emergency room bill.

4. *Major Medical:* This is designed to help pay the heavy expenses incurred during a long hospital stay due to serious illness or injury. Most major medical policies are written on a deductible basis, meaning the policyholder has to pay the first $50 to $100, or whatever amount is fixed as "deductible." Many policies also have a "co-insurance clause," meaning the policyholder also pays part of the costs above the deductible figure. For example, a policyholder with a $50 deductible and a 75 percent co-insurance clause would pay the first $50 of the bill, plus 25 percent of the total costs above that figure. Policies generally set a ceiling on maximum benefits, such as $5,000, $10,000, or $20,000. Any costs in excess of the ceiling figure would have to be paid by the policyholder.

5. *Income Protection:* This would pay a specified amount, usually not more than 75 percent of normal earnings, in weekly or monthly installments during the time the insured is away from work because of illness or injury. Policies usually place a ceiling on total benefits and require a waiting period before payments begin. The longer the waiting period, the less expensive the insurance.

Several of these five types of protection—or perhaps all of them—can be combined into one package plan usually known as a comprehensive policy.

One factor to be considered when buying health insurance is whether the company has the right to cancel the policy at any time. One of the most common types of health insurance is called the optionally renewable policy. Under this, the insurance company reserves the right to decide whether to renew the policy. More expensive is the guaranteed renewable policy. Under it, the company can increase premiums for all, or a group of its policyholders, but the policyholder's right to renew is guaranteed regardless of the number of claims he has made or the condition of his health. The most expensive type is called the noncancellable guaranteed renewable policy. As the name indicates, this policy remains in force without change so long as the policyholder pays his premiums on time.

If you are temporarily or permanently disabled because of an injury or illness related to your employment, you probably are eligible for workman's compensation benefits. State laws usually require every business establishment or employer to buy workman's compensation insurance. Maximum weekly benefits vary widely from state to state, ranging from about $20 in some states to $150 in others.

With almost all health insurance policies, benefits are curtailed at a specified age, usually sixty-five. But at this age, most individuals are eligible for Medicare.

Medicare

Medicare is a government-sponsored health insurance program for persons over sixty-five. Nearly all people sixty-five and over are eligible, including those who do not have enough credit for work covered by Social Security to qualify for monthly retirement benefits and those who had reached the age of sixty-five before the Medicare program began in July 1966.

There are two parts to Medicare. Part A provides hospital insurance to those who are eligible. Part B is a voluntary medical insurance program for those who agree to pay a specified monthly premium.

The Medicare hospital insurance program will help pay:

• A semi-private room—two to four beds in a room—and all meals, including special diets.
• Operating room charges.
• Regular nursing services, including intensive-care nursing when necessary.
• Drugs furnished by the hospital.
• X-rays and other radiology services.
• Medical supplies such as splints and casts, and the use of equipment such as wheelchairs, crutches, and braces furnished by the hospital.

For the first sixty days of hospital care, the Medicare program will pay for all but $124 of the charges for the services listed above. For the sixty-first through the ninetieth day of care, Medicare will pay for all but $31 a day of the covered services. In addition, Medicare will pay all costs over $62 a day during another sixty-day "lifetime reserve" period. These sums are subject to periodic revision.

The hospital-insurance program (Part A) does not pay for telephone, radio, or television furnished at the patient's request, private duty nurses, use of a private room—unless needed for medical reasons—and doctors' services. The voluntary medical insurance under the Medicare program (Part B) helps pay for these.

Here is an example of how Medicare helps pay for hospital care:

Mrs. Charles was in the hospital fourteen days for surgery. Her bill included the hospital charges for a semi-private room and all meals, including a special diet, use of an operating room, X-rays, laboratory tests, oxygen, and drugs furnished by the hospital. There also was a charge of $9.25 for television and telephone services. Of the total hospital bill of $789.25, Mrs. Charles paid $133.25—the $124 "deductible" plus the charges for the television and telephone. Her Medicare hospital insurance paid the remaining $656.

Monthly Social Security
Cash Benefits

(Effective June 1976)

Average yearly earnings covered by Social Security	$5,400	$6,600	$7,800	$9,000	$10,800
Retired worker 65 or older Disabled worker under 65	$319.80	$368.10	$422.40	$452.20	$490.60
Wife 65 or older	159.90	184.10	211.20	226.10	245.30
Retired worker at 62	255.90	294.50	338.00	361.80	392.50
Wife at 62, no child	120.00	138.10	158.50	169.60	184.00
Widow or widower at 65	319.80	368.10	422.40	452.20	490.60
Widow or widower at 62	265.20	305.20	350.20	375.00	406.70
Widow or widower at 60	228.70	263.20	302.10	323.40	350.80
Disabled widow or widower at 50	160.00	184.10	211.30	226.20	245.40
Wife under 65 and one child	277.30	298.40	316.90	339.20	368.00
Widowed mother and one child	479.80	552.20	633.60	678.40	736.00
Widowed mother and two children	597.00	666.30	739.20	791.70	858.60
One child of retired or disabled worker	160.00	184.10	211.30	226.20	245.40
One surviving child	239.90	276.10	316.80	339.20	368.00
Maximum family payment	597.00	666.30	739.10	791.50	858.50

Source: Social Security Administration

The medical insurance program under Medicare will help pay for medical and surgical services of a doctor regardless of where he treats you—in a hospital, his office, at a rest home, in your own home, or at a clinic. In addition, it will help pay for other services ordinarily furnished in the doctor's office and included in his bill, such as diagnostic tests, medical supplies, services of his office nurse, and drugs and medications which cannot be self-administered.

But the program does not pay for such services as routine physical checkups, examinations for eyeglasses or hearing aids, or routine dental care.

The hospital insurance is financed under the Social Security program. Employees and employers, plus self-employed persons, contribute to a special federal trust fund set up by Congress. The medical insurance is financed by the monthly premium paid by those who sign up, plus matching amounts contributed by the federal government.

Liability insurance

When planning your family's financial security, you should not overlook insurance needs other than life and health policies. Inadequate liability insurance on your automobile could result in economic disaster. *This hypothetical case shows why:*

Edward Black was driving home from vacation. It was late at night, and he was tired. He fell asleep. His car crossed the centerline of the highway and sideswiped a car going in the other direction. Mr. Black quickly regained control of his car. He was uninjured, but the other car swerved off the road and smashed into a tree, killing its four occupants. The four victims' survivors sued and won a $300,000 judgment against Mr. Black. His liability insurance covered only $50,000 of the judgment. To make up the other $250,000 he was required to turn over a substantial portion of his earnings each month for the rest of his working career.

In this age of high judgments in accident cases, family security counselors say it is prudent to carry adequate automobile liability insurance. The same holds true for liability insurance on your home. Suppose, for example, the mailman stepped on a roller skate your child left on the porch steps. The ensuing fall could result in a back injury and permanent disability for the mailman. For you it could result in a damage suit and a big judgment against you.

Most persons associate liability insurance with their automobiles or homes. You can also obtain liability protection covering accidents not related to car or home. This is usually called comprehensive personal liability. Here is an example of the protection it affords:

Suppose you were avidly casting for trout in your favorite stream when you accidentially hooked a nearby fisherman, causing a serious eye injury. A comprehensive personal liability policy would pay a damage suit award, up to limits set in the policy.

A liability policy usually pays the lawyer's fees and court costs if the policyholder is sued. These expenses alone can be substantial in prolonged litigation.

More insurance for more protection

A person of average means doesn't have the financial resources to assume the risk of losing his home, personal property, or automobile, as a result of fire, theft, or other perils. He buys insurance to protect him against these economic hazards.

For the homeowner, perhaps the most essential insurance policy protects against loss by fire. The standard policy covers both the dwelling and its contents. The "extended coverage endorsement" is a common addition to the basic fire policy. It protects against loss due to windstorms, explosions, aircraft, vehicles not owned by the insured, and other perils.

A typical theft insurance policy protects against loss of personal property to burglars who enter the premises. Jewelry and furs usually are excluded from theft coverage, unless a special clause is included at additional cost. Still another type of policy protects personal property against theft and other risks either at home or away from home. This policy lists the valuable items, such as furs, jewelry, antiques, and paintings covered. The value of each is specified, supported by an appraisal or sales receipt.

Increasing in popularity are homeowner policies, which bundle together in one package many of the types of protection available through separate policies. The package policy might include, for example, protection against the perils of fire, storm, theft, and provide personal liability coverage as well.

There are package policies, too, for the family which lives in an apartment or rented house. These are similar to homeowner policies, except coverage is limited to the contents of the building—not the building itself.

It is important to keep a full, up-to-date inventory of the contents of your home. This should include appraisals of especially valuable items. Such an inventory can help you make certain your insurance is adequate and can make it easier to prove any future property losses.

In addition to automobile liability insurance, mentioned earlier, there are other types of automobile insurance. One is a comprehensive physical damage policy that insures against such perils as fire, theft, glass breakage, wind or hail storms, and vandalism. Another type is collision insurance. This pays for damages to your car resulting from a collision with another vehicle or object—such as a tree—or occurring when your car overturns. Collision insurance does not cover personal injuries nor damage to other people's property.

Physical damage and collision insurance often are combined with liability insurance in a package policy. The package policy might also include an "uninsured motorist clause." This would protect against injury or damage caused by a hit-and-run driver, or by a driver who does not have liability insurance. Many physical damage and collision policies are written on a $50 or $100 deductible basis. This means the policyholder pays the first $50 or $100 in repair or replacement costs and the company pays the rest. As a general rule, the larger the deductible amount, the smaller the premium.

There are a number of hints which can be useful in working out your insurance problems. They are included in the next and final chapter of this section.

9

Helpful
Hints

There are a number of points in the fine print and between the lines of insurance policies which deserve close attention. If overlooked, they can prove exceedingly costly to the policyholder.

For example, if your wife should die before you do and if you fail to name one or more contingent beneficiaries, the benefits may go to your estate. There they could be subject to administrative expenses, and they may end by going to someone you may not want to have them. This points up the importance of designating contingent beneficiaries.

In event you and your wife die in the same accident, and it is established that she died even a few minutes after you did, an insurance company may have to pay the proceeds of your policy into her estate. Depending on whether she has a will and on the laws in your state, some of the money could go to her adult relatives rather than to your children.

What is known as a "common disaster clause"—included in some policies—provides protection against such an eventuality. It stipulates that the money should go into your estate unless your beneficiary—in this case, your wife—is still living a specified number of days after your death. If you name one or more contingent beneficiaries, you would have still greater protection against the danger that your insurance money will go to persons determined by a court —not by yourself.

Selecting settlement options

When you buy an insurance policy, you may select one of five settlement options which will decide the way the proceeds of your policy will be distributed. If you wish, you may leave this decision to your beneficiary to make after you die. Once you choose a settlement option, it cannot be changed by your beneficiary unless such right is specified by you in writing.

The five settlement options are:

1. *Lump sum:* The face value is paid to the beneficiary immediately upon death of the insured.

2. *Interest only:* The money may be left with the insurance company, which pays the beneficiary a guaranteed rate of interest. The interest payments may be made monthly, quarterly, semi-annually, or annually. Income tax must be paid on this interest, except for a $1,000 annual exemption when it is paid in installments to a surviving spouse.

Under this option, the policyholder may specify that the policy proceeds be held by the company until a certain date. This would enable you, for example, to make certain that a college fund is there when your children need it. On the other hand, the policyholder can give the beneficiary the right to withdraw the full proceeds at any time. Or he may grant the beneficiary the right to withdraw a certain amount, say $1,000 in any one year. This would allow some of the proceeds to be used in an emergency without the temptation of full withdrawal.

3. *Limited installments:* You may direct that proceeds be paid to the beneficiary in regular installments, usually monthly, for a certain number of years. For instance, if you specified that your $20,000 death benefit be paid to your widow over a ten-year period, she would receive $185 each month. Altogether, she would receive more than $22,000, the extra $2,000 representing interest paid by the insurance company.

4. *Fixed income:* You may direct the insurance company to pay your beneficiary a certain amount at regular intervals, such as $100 each month, until proceeds of the policy are exhausted. For example if you directed that the proceeds of a $20,000 policy be paid to your widow at the rate of $100 a month, she would receive payments for more than twenty-one years. The payments would total about $25,000 with interest paid by the insurance company accounting for the extra $5,000.

5. *Life income:* If you select this option, the insurance company agrees to pay equal monthly installments to the beneficiary for life. Under some plans, you may specify that if the beneficiary dies within a certain period, such as twenty years, the payments would be continued in favor of a second beneficiary. The size of the monthly installments depends on the age of the beneficiary. If he is young and likely to collect for a long time, they could be small. If he is older, they would be larger. For example, if you have a $20,000 policy and you die when your wife is forty years old, she might receive about $65 a month for the rest of her life. But if your wife is sixty years old, she might receive about $110 a month for life.

If you examine your life insurance policy, you should find

charts illustrating the varying payments under the different options. If the information is not contained in the policy, it can be obtained from the insurance company.

Options on dividends

If you own a participating life insurance policy, your annual premium is set at a rate higher than the company expects will be needed to meet operating expenses. At the end of the year, this overpayment is returned to you in the form of dividends. Usually you can select one of these five ways to receive the dividends:

1. You may take the dividends in cash.

2. You may use the dividends to reduce premiums. If you select this option, the company deducts the dividend from your next premium and you pay only the difference.

3. You may leave the dividends with the company to accumulate interest. The dividends and accumulated interest can be withdrawn at any time.

4. You may use your dividends to purchase paid-up permanent life insurance. This means the total face value of the insurance continues to increase each year. Selection of this option would be one way to offset the eroding effect inflation has on life insurance values. But it should be selected only if you want additional insurance.

5. You may direct that your dividends be used to buy a one-year term insurance policy. This additional policy would expire after one year, but the next year's dividend would purchase another term policy. Remember, premiums on term insurance increase as you get older. But often the dividends paid on an insurance policy increase the longer that it is held.

Adding value to your policy

For additional premiums, most life insurance companies will attach to their policies a variety of provisions giving the policyholder extra benefits or options. These special clauses are known as "riders." Some riders have become so common they are automatically inserted into a policy, and the premium quoted includes the extra cost.

Some of the riders found most often in life insurance policies are:

• *Double indemnity:* With this clause, your beneficiary would receive twice the policy's face value should you die in an accident, or within a specified time, such as ninety days, after being injured in an accident. For example, if you own a $10,000 life insurance policy with a double indemnity rider and you are fatally injured in an automobile accident, your family would receive death benefits of $20,000. Some companies offer triple indemnity riders which pay three times the face value in the event of accidental death.

Since the additional cost of a double indemnity clause usually is small, many persons feel the extra protection is a bargain. But is it? The chances are small that you will die as the result of an accident. And the financial needs of your family will be the same, whether you die in an accident or from other causes. If you have an insurance program that adequately covers your family's needs, then the double indemnity rider may be unnecessary. If additional protection is advisable, then the money you would spend for the rider might better be spent on expanding the family's basic insurance program.

• *Disability waiver:* Under this rider, the insurance company will pay the premiums on your policy if you become totally and permanently disabled. Your policy would remain in force just as if you were paying the premiums. Cash values would continue to increase, dividends would be paid to you, and the death benefits would remain the same. Without such a clause, many persons who become disabled would be unable to continue their insurance program. The cost of this "insurance on insurance" is low, often less than a dollar a year for each $1,000 of insurance. Most disability waivers contain several limitations. You usually are not considered permanently disabled until you have been off work for six months. Total disability is defined as your inability to engage in any occupation for gain or profit.

• *Guaranteed insurability:* Under this clause, which is relatively new, you reserve the right to purchase additional protection or policies at specified dates in the future without taking a medical examination. Here is an example of how this rider works:

John Smith, twenty-three, purchased a $10,000 whole life policy. For an additional premium of less than $15 a year, the company added a rider to the policy guaranteeing that he could purchase additional $10,000 policies at ages twenty-five, twenty-eight, thirty-one, thirty-four, thirty-seven, and forty without proving he was in good health. If John discovers at age twenty-seven that he has a chronic illness which ordinarily would make him uninsurable, he still can purchase an additional $50,000 in protection by age forty under the guaranteed insurability rider.

Coverage limitations

When you read your life insurance policy, you will notice several paragraphs that limit the policy's coverage. For example, a limitation found in many policies is called the "suicide clause." It states that if the policyholder commits suicide within a specified period of time after the policy is issued—usually two or three years—the company will not pay death benefits, but instead will return the amount of premiums paid on the policy. This clause obviously is designed to prevent people who are contemplating suicide from purchasing large amounts of insurance in advance.

Many policies include a "war clause" stating that death benefits will not be paid if death results from an act of war. Inclusion of this clause in policies was one of the rea-

sons why the federal government offered life insurance pol
icies to military personnel during World War I, World War
II, and the Korean War. Still other clauses may disallow
payment of death benefits if death results from an accident
involving an aircraft other than a scheduled airliner, or if
death results from committing or attempting to commit a
crime.

Your life insurance policy also probably contains a para-
graph stating that, after the policy has been in force for a
certain period of time—usually one or two years—it shall
be "incontestable" by the company for any cause. During
the specified period, the company has a chance to check the
information you gave in applying for the policy. After the
specified time elapses, the company cannot cancel the policy
on grounds the application contained a misstatement.

Life insurance and taxes

As a general rule, the entire lump sum of life insurance
policy proceeds payable at an insured person's death is
exempt from federal income tax, whether the sum is payable to an individual or to the insured person's estate.

When death benefits are paid in installments rather than
in a lump sum, taxes are due on that part of each payment
attributable to interest received from the insurance company. When the beneficiary is the surviving spouse, taxes
are paid only when the total interest exceeds $1,000 a year.

For example, in the year following her husband's death,
Ruth Smith received a total of $4,000 in monthly install-
ments from an insurance company. Of this, $3,500 came
from principal and $500 from interest paid by the com-
pany. This $500 in interest is tax free for the widow, since
it is below the $1,000 exemption. The $3,500 paid from the
principal is tax free, too.

When proceeds of a policy are left on deposit with the insurance company and the company makes interest payments to the beneficiary, that interest is taxable. Once

again, the $1,000 annual exemption applies if interest payments go to a surviving spouse. No additional taxes are incurred when the principal is eventually handed over to the beneficiary.

Part of the cash surrender values that build up in permanent insurance policies may, in some instances, be considered taxable income. This can happen when the cash value exceeds the total premiums paid on a policy. For example, suppose you own a policy on which you have paid a total of $10,000 in premiums. Over the years, the policy's cash values has built up to $11,000. If you surrender the policy and receive the $11,000, the excess over the premiums you have paid—in this case $1,000—would be considered taxable income.

Normally, when you exchange property rights for other property rights, you must pay taxes on any gain. For instance, if you sell shares of a stock at a profit, you must pay a tax even though you promptly invest the proceeds in other stock. This provision does not apply to insurance. You can exchange one insurance policy for another without being liable for taxes.

Ways of shielding the proceeds of insurance from the impact of estate taxes will be considered in the next section.

Here are some basic pointers for policyholders:

1. *Read your policy.* Be sure you understand the extent of its coverage, the amount of benefits, plus any limitations and restrictions. Your agent can answer any questions you might have. You can write to the company or to your state insurance department.

2. *Discuss your insurance program with your family.* It is best to have your family or other beneficiaries share in the planning of your life insurance program. Discuss with them any additions or revisions in the program. You might also want to leave a letter stating where the policies are

kept, outlining the benefits and explaining the choices the beneficiary may have in the settlement of policies.

3. *Keep your policy in a safe place.* Your insurance company will issue a duplicate policy if yours is lost or destroyed by fire. But there could be some delay, and this could come at an already trying time for your family since the policy generally must be presented with requests for benefits. If you keep your policy in a safe deposit box, remember this: In some states the safe deposit box of a person who dies may be opened only by court order. Even his widow could be prohibited from opening it.

4. *Keep the company informed of your address.* Insurance companies say some policyholders move without notifying them or leaving a forwarding address. This could cause you to miss a dividend check, or it could cause a lapse in your policy if you miss a premium due notice.

5. *Review your insurance program periodically.* A life insurance program purchased by a man twenty-five years old may not fit his needs at age forty, and it almost certainly won't when he reaches age sixty. You should review your insurance program every few years.

CHAPTER 10

Making
Your Will

Some day everything you own, all the worldly possessions that you may have worked hard to accumulate, will pass to others. They could conceivably go to the wrong people, or they could be drained away by taxes and expenses.

That need not happen. A few relatively simple precautions described in this and succeeding chapters, can help you safeguard your estate for those you would like to inherit it.

The first and most important step is to proceed without further delay in drawing up a will, if you do not have one. If you do have one, then you should proceed to review it in the light of today's changed circumstances.

Through a will you can command the disposition of your possessions as you desire. In the absence of a will, you lose the power to command and it is left to others, notably the courts, to dispose of your possessions according to state laws. In this circumstance, you may unwittingly injure those most dear to you and help those who are of no particular interest to you.

Your property may even go to people you wouldn't want to have it, or there may be unnecessary red tape in distributing your assets. And there may be extra expenses that could have been avoided.

Many believe that wills and "estate plans" are for the rich—only for those who have "estates." This may explain the extraordinary fact that seven out of eight adults in the United States fail to make a will.

But anyone who owns anything holds something of value. And if he has someone he would like to leave it to, he cannot be absolutely sure it will get to that person unless he takes the trouble of putting his wishes down on paper in a properly prepared will.

Furthermore, many people possess more than they are aware of—perhaps a home, a car, some life insurance, a savings account. Others may also have some group insurance, pension rights, an interest in a company, union, or government retirement plan.

To accumulate his estate—and every man has an estate, large or small—the average American spends a lifetime. Yet the majority of these average Americans never get around to spending the little time necessary to insure that their estates will be passed on to those of their choice.

When there is no will

Every week in recent years, nearly $100 million in cash and other assets, left by people who die without wills, pile up in state probate courts. Additional millions are tied up in legal snarls when wills are outdated or unclear.

When a person fails to make a will, or has a will which for some reason is held invalid, then that person is said to die "intestate." The state government, in effect, writes a will for him. His real estate is distributed according to the laws of the state where the property is located. His personal property is distributed according to the laws of the state where he lived.

One expert on estate planning explains it this way:

"In one sense, everybody has a will. If you don't provide one, the state—by your default—does so under its statutes of descent. The question is whether you are willing to settle for this assemblyline way of passing along your property that must ignore individual desires."

The rules for distribution of the estate of one who does not leave a will vary widely from state to state. Generally, they attempt to favor the surviving spouse and children. But there have been many cases where property went to more distant heirs who would not have received it if the owner had made careful plans.

Many people think a wife automatically inherits everything when the husband dies. This is not so. If there is no will, the wife in most states receives from one-third to one-half of the estate. In some states, the wife's share is equal to a child's share. If, for example, there are four children, the widow gets only one-fifth of the estate. The rest is equally divided among the children.

Children under twenty-one years of age cannot accept their share of the estate in their own right. Their share must go into a trust, or its distribution must be under an adult's control. Chances are the widow would be appointed trustee or distributor of the funds, but she would be restricted to spending the money only for the children. In most cases, it would be better if the wife had control of the full amount, with no strings attached. This would enable her to cope with any sudden family emergency, such as a serious illness and the resulting medical expense.

The appointment of a trustee or a guardian to oversee

distribution of a child's share of an estate can be cumbersome, even if the widow is appointed. Some states require the trustee to be bonded and insist upon judicial approval before any of a child's share of an estate can be spent. A mother might discover that, to use estate funds for the child's college tuition, she must bring a court proceeding for authorization. As a mother, she may know best, but her actions are subject to judicial supervision.

Even when children are grown, lack of a will can create problems. An attorney tells of a widow compelled in her sixties to take a job. It was the last thing her husband would have wanted, but he never got around to making a will.

The couple's two children were married and self supporting. The husband assumed his $100,000 estate would go to his wife. But in the absence of a will and under state law the wife received only one-third of the estate. Part of this share was in stocks and real estate she could not turn into cash without the consent of the children. These children were prepared to take care of their mother. Not all children are. This mother wanted her independence. She went to work when she might have been enjoying retirement.

If there are no children, intestate laws in some states specify that the wife will receive a certain amount, such as the first $5,000 plus one-half of the remainder of the estate. Under this system, in the case of a $25,000 estate, the wife would receive the first $5,000 plus one-half of the balance, or an additional $10,000. The parents of the deceased would receive the remaining $10,000. If both parents were dead, the $10,000 would be distributed to surviving brothers and sisters. But if no brothers or sisters survived, the money could go to nieces or nephews of the husband, or perhaps even some more distant relative, leaving his wife in desperate financial straits.

One estate planner gives this example of what can happen:

A successful corporation executive died unexpectedly without leaving a will. His only surviving relatives were his wife and a niece he had not seen in twenty years. Because he did not leave a will, state law governed distribution of his estate. His widow received the first $5,000 and was forced to share the balance of his estate with the niece.

Recognizing this as an injustice, some states have enacted laws giving the widow a large maximum dollar amount if there are no children. In Massachusetts and New York, for example, the widow would receive $25,000, plus one-half of the remainder of the estate.

Laws in most states specify that if the spouse does not survive, then the children have the next priority. But what happens if the children die before their parents? In such a case, the grandchildren will share in the estate. But states differ as to how. A few states specify that distribution be "per stirpes," or by roots. Most others specify that it will be "per capita," or by head.

Under the per capita plan, the grandchildren would share equally. The per stirpes method gives an equal share in each branch of the family. Thus if a man had two sons who raised families and died before he did, his estate would be divided into two parts. Half the estate would go to the children of one son, half to the children of the other. Under this system, the only child of one son would get as much as the six children of another would share.

In addition to problems of distribution, the cost of administering an estate may be greater when there is no will. In most states, the administrator of an intestate estate must furnish a bond. While this protects beneficiaries and creditors of the estate, the cost of the premiums must be paid either out of the estate or out of the administrator's fees. Often the administrator must seek court authorization before he can sell property, compromise claims, or distribute the estate.

These restrictions are intended to protect the assets in

an estate, but sometimes they can hinder sound management of those same assets. For example, some states limit administrators to specified types of investments. The estate may include a block of "blue chip" common stock, but if the laws of the state do not permit investment in common stock, then the administrator would have to sell—even if it meant a loss for the estate. The court expenses which result from such required judicial proceedings must be paid by the estate.

If you die without a will, the court selects the administrator of your estate. Generally, the surviving spouse—husband or wife—has the first right to be appointed. But in some cases this might not be desirable. The widow, for example, might not have the experience or knowledge to manage the estate efficiently. If there is no surviving spouse, or if the spouse does not want to be administrator, the courts usually turn next to the children. Sometimes, if they are of age, the court will appoint all the children to serve jointly as administrators. This can cause problems.

The seven children of an attorney quarreled endlessly about the administration of his estate. All wanted a voice in decisions. None wanted the responsibility involved in overseeing the estate. While the estate stagnated, they blamed each other for lack of initiative, and each complained he could do nothing. The result? Inefficient and costly administration of the estate.

What a will can do

These have been some of the difficulties encountered when a person dies without a will. Consider the advantages that flow from making a will and keeping it up to date.

You can make certain the proceeds of your estate are distributed according to your wishes.

You can appoint your own executor.

You can select guardians for surviving minor children.

You can hold down the costs of administering your estate.

You can arrange for cash to be made available to pay debts and take care of your expenses.

You can specify charities and individuals outside your immediate family to whom you might want to make some bequests.

If you have a will, you not only can specify the beneficiaries but you can also determine what share of the estate they will get. You might, for example, want one child to receive more than other children in the family. This could be true in the case of a disabled or handicapped child. Without a will, all children would be treated alike because your estate would be distributed according to state laws. The healthy, able children would receive the same share as their less fortunate brother or sister.

Under most state laws, a spouse cannot be disinherited. Generally, he or she is entitled to at least one-third of the estate, sometimes one-half. In some states, however, a will can specify that this portion be placed in trust and that the surviving spouse receive only the income from it.

With a will, you can make bequests to charities, to your church, or to a long-time friend. This is impossible to do without a will, since the laws of intestacy provide for distribution of an estate only to relatives.

In case your spouse does not survive you, experts say you should name in your will a guardian of your minor children, those under twenty-one. To cover the event that one guardian might become ill or die, you might consider naming an alternate guardian. Experts advise: Don't decide upon a guardian until you and your husband or wife thoroughly discuss who is best qualified and until those you choose agree to accept the responsibility of raising the children and managing the property you leave them.

In a will, you can name the person you want to administer your estate. By selecting this executor—executrix if female—in advance, you can speed up and simplify the distribution of your estate.

How should you choose an executor for your will?

The tendency often is to name a friend or relative. But estate planning authorities say that unless your estate is extremely small and uncomplicated, the best bet might be to pick a specialist. Handling even a small estate can be an extremely technical job, with pitfalls awaiting the amateur.

In recent years, there has been a trend toward naming a bank or a trust company as executor. A bank or trust company is a continuing organization which will be in existence long after an individual executor might become unavailable. In addition, a bank or trust company offers full-time management by experts.

A possible disadvantage is that a bank or trust company cannot take the personal interest that might be expected of a friend or relative. A compromise is possible. To obtain the experienced management of a bank or trust company and the personal touch of a friend or relative, you could appoint coexecutors. The bank or trust company could handle the more technical aspects, such as investments. The friend or relative could have certain powers over the way the estate is distributed.

In most cases, the scale of fees banks and trust companies charge for their services is fixed by state law or by the courts. Generally, this amounts to a percentage of the income from the property or a percentage of the principal of the estate, or both.

In one eastern state, for example, the law permits an executor to charge up to 10 percent of the first $20,000 of the gross assets in the estate, plus 4 percent of the balance. In this case, the maximum fee of an executor on a $50,000 estate would be $3,200. In many cases it is less. Remember that the assets in such an estate exclude jointly held property, life insurance proceeds, or trust assets.

When a friend or relative is named executor, he often serves without fee. Even so, some estate planners say, this person can be the most expensive executor. One case history illustrates:

When a businessman died, his son was named executor, as specified in his will. The son sold his father's business, receiving $200,000 in cash to be distributed to heirs. But because of his inexperience, it took more than three years to distribute the estate's assets. During this time, the sum received from the sale of the business was held in cash. Had it been invested, the estate would have earned about $25,000 in gross income. In this case, the cash earned nothing.

With a few sentences in your will, you can trim estate administration expenses. For example, you could dispense with the requirement that your executor be bonded. In a small estate, this could save several hundred dollars. In a larger estate, the savings could be in the thousands of dollars. With your will, you also can broaden the powers of the executor. For instance, you can give him authority to sell real estate and thus save the cost of a court proceeding for judicial approval. Such authority for your executor could be important, especially if there were a need to convert some assets of the estate into cash to pay debts and cover expenses.

Women and wills

Both husband and wife should have a will. Many women fail to draw up wills because they think they have little property. Nonetheless, the wife can arrange to "thoughtfully dispose" of such personal belongings as jewelry, antiques, paintings, furs, and other items. Only a will can assure that such property goes directly to the intended beneficiary.

A wife may acquire property unexpectedly through gifts

or inheritance. In the event of her husband's death, she could receive a sizeable amount of property. But unless she has a will, her death would thwart any plan the couple might have had for the distribution of their combined property.

This case demonstrates why a wife should have a will:

A widower with two young daughters married for the second time. He revised his will, leaving all his property to his new wife, assuming that in case of his death she would continue to look after her stepdaughters.

Soon after this marriage, the man and his new wife were fatally injured in an automobile crash. The husband died instantly; his wife, a few days later.

Under terms of the husband's will, all of his property passed to his wife. But she had no will. Upon her death, their combined property wound up in court for distribution. State law gave the entire estate to relatives of the second wife. Since his daughters were not related to her by blood, they were left with no inheritance.

What would have happened to the estate if the husband and wife had both died instantly in the accident?

In the event of simultaneous deaths, if there are no wills, the joint property is divided in half, and each half is distributed according to the laws of their state. If, for example, the estate totaled $50,000, it would be split $25,000 in the husband's estate and $25,000 in the wife's estate. The husband's daughters probably would receive $25,000 from their father's estate, but the other $25,000 would go to the wife's relatives.

Two variations of the standard will are the joint will and the mutual will. Here's how they differ: A joint will is one document drawn up and signed by two persons, usually husband and wife. Mutual wills are separate documents executed by two persons, again usually husband and wife, with both containing similar or reciprocal provisions.

A common purpose of a joint will is to facilitate the transfer of property owned jointly by husband and wife. Another purpose is to provide one estate plan which is complete and constant. Often the couple believes a joint will makes things simpler. But most estate planners caution that such wills can complicate proceedings. They obviously are more complex than individual wills. Courts have, on occasion, rejected joint wills unless they were perfectly clear.

Drawing up a will

All states set a minimum age for making a valid will. Some, such as Massachusetts, fix the age at twenty-one. Others, like California, specify eighteen. New York fixes the age at twenty-one for real property and eighteen for personal property. In some states the minimum age for men is twenty-one, while for women it is eighteen.

Most states also require that the person who makes a will be of "sound mind." This has been interpreted as meaning that a person understands he is making a will, that he knows without prompting the extent of his property, and that he realizes his relationship to others who might share in his estate.

Because a will is a legal document, there are certain formalities that usually must be observed in order for it to be valid. One general rule is that the person making out the will sign it in ink immediately after the last sentence in the body of the will. His signature should be exactly as his name appears in the will, and his signature or initials should also be placed on each of the other pages of the will.

The will must be signed in the presence of the required number of witnesses. In some states, the requirement is two witnesses; in others, it is three. The spouse of the person making the will should not act as a witness. Nor should any person who is named as a beneficiary in the will. If the beneficiary signs as a witness, he may lose what has been left him in the will. The witnesses need not read the will before they sign, but the maker of the will, the testator, should tell them it is his last will and testament.

Seek professional help

To be effective, a will must comply precisely with state law. While there is no legal requirement that a will be drawn by a lawyer, you would be courting trouble not to use one. Most laymen are unfamiliar with the mandatory and exacting formalities of the law.

The cost of having a will prepared varies widely, depending on the amount of property involved, the complexity of the document and the time it takes the lawyer to do the job. The cost of drawing a simple will for a man of modest means might run between $50 and $100. Preparation of a more complicated will involving elaborate estate planning may run into hundreds of dollars. Legal authorities suggest that you discuss fees with your lawyer in advance.

Don't let inertia or fear of extra expense deter you from making changes in a will if circumstances call for them. The cost of not making the change could be far greater.

Should your will require only minor revisions, your lawyer probably would add a "codicil," modifying some of the original provisions. Since this becomes a part of the will, it should be executed formally. You should not try to handle it yourself by typing a section onto the original document. This could cause a court to throw out the entire will. If major changes are needed, your lawyer undoubtedly will suggest that a new will be drawn.

How often should your will be updated?

Experts say wills should be reviewed at least once a year. But they add that the lapse of time in itself is no yardstick. It may be that the document prepared twenty years ago is still adequate to meet today's needs or that the will executed only six months ago already is outdated.

Here are some questions you might ask yourself in determining whether your will needs to be updated:

—Have you had a new child? In some states, the birth of a child after a parent has drawn a will can mean the complete revocation of the will. In most states, the law provides that when a child is born after a will is made, that child is entitled to take his "intestate share" in the same manner as if no will existed. Here's an illustration of the problems this could cause: Suppose a man with two children executed a will leaving everything to his wife. If a new child was born after the will was drawn, and the will was not revised, the new child might receive a portion of the estate, but the two older children would not.

—Have there been other changes in your family status? Suppose your will provided a lump-sum payment of $25,000 for an elderly aunt. If the aunt died, you would need to revise your will and arrange for that money to go to someone else.

—Have you moved to a new state? In today's mobile society, when companies routinely transfer executives and employees from coast to coast, you should have your will examined by an attorney if you change residence. The laws which governed your will when you were living in one state may or may not hold in your new state of residence.

—Has your financial status changed? Any substantial ups or downs in your financial condition may make a review of the terms of your will advisable.

—Have the needs of your beneficiaries changed? Suppose, since you executed your will, one of your three sons has developed a chronic illness that will keep him from making the same financial progress in life as his brothers. You probably would want to revise your will to make special provisions for his needs.

—Have you disposed of property specifically bequeathed in your will? If this has happened, you may wish to substitute other property. Many an intended beneficiary has been denied an inheritance because specific property he was left in a will had been sold or in some way altered, and the will had not been updated.

—Have there been changes in the tax laws? There are periodic revisions in state and federal laws governing the taxation of estates and trusts. Your lawyer would know whether your will needs to be changed to prevent unnecessary taxation.

Experts also suggest:

A copy of your will should be kept in a safe but accessible place at home, along with information where the original is. The original may be left with the lawyer who drew it, with your bank, or with the person named as executor. If you keep the original copy of your will in a safe deposit box, there might be delay in getting it out. Most states seal such boxes upon death and permit them to be opened only by court order.

It is a good idea to leave with your lawyer or executor a letter of instruction to become effective only upon your death. Such a letter is not legally binding, but it could contain information that would be useful to your family. It might contain information on the location of the will and other important documents, such as your birth certificate, Social Security card, insurance policies, marriage certificate, and Armed Forces discharge papers.

11

Bypassing "Probate"

Probate is the legal procedure for validating a will and thereby permitting it to come into operation. It also covers the entire process of settling an estate in accordance with the wishes of its owner.

The intervention of a court in matters of this kind is to the legitimate interest of the principals involved, above all the author of the will. A court must determine that the will is authentic—that it is, in fact, the maker's last will and testament.

However, the entire process of "admitting a will to probate"—that is, securing the court's stamp of approval—is usually a complicated and lengthy one. It can also be costly because of all the administrative and legal fees involved. And it can result in higher taxes than need be paid.

Consequently, an increasing number of people have been

looking for ways "to avoid probate." Actually, it is not possible for a will to avoid probate. A will cannot come into operation without going through the legal process.

However, it is possible to make arrangements whereby important parts of your estate may bypass the probate process. There is no law that says you must dispose of all your possessions exclusively through provisions in a will. You have a perfect right, in fact, to keep some of the assets of your estate out of the hands of the court and out of the probate process so as to save time, trouble, and taxes for your heirs.

In most jurisdictions, the court that handles estate matters is called probate court. In some areas it is known as surrogate, chancery, county, or orphan's court.

After the court is satisfied that your document complies with state laws and admits your will to probate, it qualifies an executor and issues what are called letters testamentary so that he can administer and settle the estate.

One of his first tasks is to collect and preserve your property, then have it appraised. An inventory of your property, along with the appraised values, is submitted to the court and the taxing authorities. To notify creditors and others who might have a claim against your estate, the executor places a legal notice in the newspaper. Claims generally must be filed with the executor within six to nine months after the estate proceeding starts. Claims not filed within that time generally are held invalid. Since unforeseen creditors might file a claim just before the deadline, the estate usually is kept "open" until the filing time has passed. Once the deadline has passed and all justified claims—and estate taxes—have been paid, the executor parcels out the rest of your property to the persons or institutions named in your will. All along, he is making periodic reports to the probate court, which audits his transactions. The executor's job ends when he makes his final accounting of the distribution of the estate to the court.

Even with a simple will, this process often takes more than a year to complete. With a complicated will, the settlement may drag on for several years—particularly if there are securities to be sold or a business to liquidate. In one Maryland case, a widow complained that the $150,000 estate of her husband, who had died in 1955, was still unsettled in 1963.

The probate process can be expensive too. In some cases, administrative fees and expenses can bite 10 percent or more from the value of an estate.

If the executor of your estate is not a lawyer, he probably will have to hire one. Regardless of how your estate is arranged, there will be legal work to be done. There are other expenses, such as appraiser's fees and charges for filing documents in court.

The high cost of probate has caused such a furor in some areas that a committee of legal experts set out to draft a "model probate code" aimed at standardizing fees and eliminating questionable practices.

Besides the delays and the expense, the probate process can bring publicity. Nearly every newspaper has a reporter assigned to cover probate court, and, since all court documents are open for public inspection, there probably would be news stories about any large or interesting estate.

If delay, expense, and possible publicity trouble you, remember this: Not everything you possess has to go through the probate process—only those assets which are covered by the will.

There are several ways to see that your beneficiaries get property without putting it through the probate process. But counselors stress this point: Seek professional help—don't try to do the job yourself. An attorney who specializes in estate practice can help you figure out how some of your assets may be kept out of the probate process. He is familiar with the whole picture, and can give you maximum protection against possible pitfalls.

Trusts, which can be created during one's lifetime, can transfer property outside your will. Property can be placed in joint ownership, with the survivor automatically becoming the sole owner. Life insurance proceeds also go directly to a named beneficiary. So do death benefits under a qualified profit-sharing or pension plan.

But perhaps the simplest method of bypassing the probate system is to give away some of your assets during your lifetime. In brief, estate planners say that making gifts to people as you go through life has a double advantage: it makes cash or other property available at once to those who will benefit from it, and sometimes it can mean a savings in taxes since it keeps assets from piling up in your estate.

Until 1976 the federal tax on gifts was lower than the federal tax on estates. But Congress changed the law and made the two rates the same. The changes in the tax law are discussed in detail in the next chapter, including important exemptions and exclusions which still make it possible for people to give away substantial sums of money or property during their lifetime without incurring any tax liability.

Now, let's examine some of the more common ways to bypass the probate process.

Setting up trusts

Trusts once were regarded as useful only for millionaires or those with complicated estates. But in recent years more and more individuals, including many with relatively small estates, have discovered that trusts offer advantages in passing along part of their property to their heirs. Depending on its type and structure, a trust may reduce the income tax liability of the person establishing the trust, reduce the ultimate tax on his estate, or both.

Trusts known as "lifetime trusts" are favored by some because they can be set up and carried out in privacy. Only the principals involved and the tax authorities need know a trust has been created. By contrast, a trust that is set up in a will, known as a "testamentary trust," is open to public inspection once the will is put on file in the probate court.

A word of caution: A person planning to set up a trust would be wise to consult with experts, such as a lawyer or accountant. These specialists can outline the legal and tax aspects, and, if you decide to establish a trust, they can help make certain the proper procedures are followed.

Stripped of technicalities, a trust is simply an arrangement whereby legal title to property is transferred to another person, or to a trust company. The trustee holds, invests, and administers the property for the benefit of the persons, charities, or institutions designated as beneficiaries.

The different kinds of trusts we mentioned are the two basic ones. The "lifetime trust" gets its name from the fact that it is established and becomes operative during one's lifetime. The "testamentary trust," set up under a will—a "testament"—becomes effective only upon the death of the person who drew the will.

The lifetime trust, also known in legal terminology as an "inter vivos" trust, can be either revocable or irrevocable. The revocable trust can be revoked at the option of the person who created it. Its provisions can be changed, or the trust can be terminated in whole or in part, at any time. In contrast, the irrevocable trust, once it is set up, must run unchanged for a specified term. The person who set it up cannot change his mind in midstream.

Generally speaking, current tax benefits come only under the irrevocable trust. Income taxes can be reduced when the income of the trust is taxable to a beneficiary, such as a child or an elderly person, who is in a lower tax bracket than the person who created the trust. Estate taxes are reduced because the property is removed permanently from the estate of the person who set up the trust.

But these tax advantages must be weighed carefully

against possible disadvantages. For example, tax authorities and others caution against making binding trust arrangements that may be regretted later. At some future time, you might need the use of the property you have tied up irrevocably.

What is the best way to set up a trust?

The possibilities are countless. The following is one method that is becoming increasingly popular among estate planners:

A married man who wants to leave property to his wife and children establishes a lifetime trust in two parts. One part is called a "marital trust;" the other, a "residuary trust." Upon the husband's death, the wife gets the income from both trusts. She can also draw on the principal of the marital trust if she needs extra income. The marital trust property is not subject to taxation at the time of the husband's death. It is included in the taxable estate of the wife when she dies. If the residuary trust is properly designed, its property is taxed at the husband's death, but it is not taxed again at the wife's death. The principal of the residuary trust passes along to the children. Both trusts, while subject to some taxes, bypass the probate process.

There also is one type of trust that makes possible immediate tax savings, without requiring the person who sets up the trust to lose control forever of the property he places in the trust. Known as the "reversionary trust," it is an irrevocable trust for a definite period of time—not less than 10 years unless the person receiving income from the trust dies before the end of the specified period. At the end of the specified period, the trust property reverts back to the person who created the trust.

Here's an example of how the reversionary trust can be used:

Suppose a young business executive has $10,000 invested

in securities as part of his retirement plan. If he is in the 50 percent income tax bracket, he is able under normal circumstances to retain only half the income. If the income is $400, he keeps only about $200. But if he sets up a reversionary trust to run for at least ten years, the tax on that same income, if it is accumulated within the trust, would be $28—instead of $200. Thus, the trust would accumulate $372 a year, or $3,720 over a ten-year period. If he wished, he could arrange to make a gift of the income to his retired father.

There are several points to remember about reversionary trusts. First, the income from the trust cannot be used to meet a legal obligation of the person who set up the trust. For example, the income cannot be used to support a minor child. It could, however, be used to help finance a college education for that same child.

Keep in mind, too, that a reversionary trust is a gift of income, not of principal. In most cases, there are no estate tax advantages, since the property comes back at the end of the specified period.

Trust provisions often can be kept flexible enough to cover many contingencies that can not be foreseen.

Suppose, for example, that you leave $100,000 in a lifetime trust for your wife, with the provision that it be divided among your children upon her death.

You may not want to decide in advance precisely how much each child is to get. It's possible that one child will have an accident or develop a crippling disease which would make him more dependent on your money than the other children would be.

By giving your wife "power of appointment" in the trust agreement, you can delegate to her the right to stipulate in her will exactly how much money each child is to receive after her death.

A trust also can include clauses to safeguard what you consider the best interests of your beneficiaries. For instance, a man might leave money in trust for a son's widow, but specify that if she remarries, his grandchildren will get the money instead.

For people with considerable wealth to pass along, a "charitable trust" can be useful in reducing estate taxes. The donor removes the gift from his estate by establishing a trust. The principal is placed in reserve for a university, charity, or other nonprofit organization. The donor can arrange to receive the income for his lifetime, after which the income goes to his wife for her lifetime. When both have died, the principal goes to the beneficiary.

Another type of trust—the life insurance trust—can be set up by making a trustee, usually a bank or trust company, the beneficiary of a life insurance policy or policies. Upon death, the proceeds of the insurance policies are invested and installment payments are made to the wife and children of the insured. This procedure keeps insurance benefits from being dissipated within a few years, as often happens when proceeds are paid in a lump sum.

When the amount of insurance involved is relatively small, experts say it is not advisable to set up a life insurance trust. For example, the income from the investment of the proceeds of a $10,000 policy would yield, assuming a 5 percent return, only about $500 a year—obviously inadequate to support a widow and children. In such a case, it usually is best to have the proceeds paid directly to the beneficiary. If a much larger sum, such as $100,000 is involved, then the return on the investment might provide sufficient income for a widow.

You can specify in your insurance policy that the proceeds be paid to the beneficiary in regular installments, or that the proceeds be held by the insurance company and a regular rate of interest be paid the beneficiary. Such an arrangement could accomplish the same objective as a life insurance trust, with this advantage. It would be cheaper, since the insurance company makes no charge for handling the proceeds in this way, while a bank or trust company would charge a fee. However, the life insurance trust can provide greater flexibility, since you can give the bank or trust company discretion to use the principal to augment the income earned through investments.

If you are considering setting up any type of trust, experts say it generally is advisable to include language providing for "invasion of trust." This would allow withdrawal of a portion of the principal to meet medical bills or the cost of education.

As one expert noted: "There's always danger of tying up your property so tight that you can't get at it in case of some dire need. Some people would rather pay out more in taxes and have control of their money while they are alive. Others may be more intent on saving taxes. Both these positions have merit. It's up to the individual to decide what is best for him, taking all factors into account."

Selecting a trustee

If you decide to set up a trust, you face another important decision: Whom should you select as trustee?

Before you pick a trustee, you should make certain he can handle the job. A trustee may have to make repeated investments over the years, make accountings to the beneficiaries, file income taxes for the trust every year, and exercise his own discretion as to the distribution of trust funds to beneficiaries.

While an executor's job is over in a few years at most, the trustee probably will have to act over a long period of time. An estate might require trustees for seventy-five years, with the financial security of several generations involved. To assure continuity, you may want to choose a trust company or a bank as trustee. As a possible compromise, you could name an individual and a trust company as cotrustees. As a third possibility, you could name an individual as trustee with the provision that a specified corporate trustee would take over when the individual trustee dies. If you don't select such a successor trustee, the courts would make the choice for you.

Trustees, whether individual or corporate, are entitled to compensation for their work. The fees, or the method of calculating them, usually are determined by state law or court decisions. The rates vary from state to state, but generally are based on the principal amount invested and the annual income of the trust. In most states, a sliding scale is used, with the percentage fee being smaller as the size of the trust increases.

Various state laws give some assurance of safety to all persons involved in a trust. In general, these laws require that a trustee keep accurate accounts of the assets, which must be segregated; that he comply with the wishes of the person who set up the trust; and that he take no personal advantage of his position.

Except in the cases of charitable or employee trusts, no state will allow a trust to operate indefinitely. In most states, a trust cannot extend beyond the lifetime of a reasonable number of "named" persons living at the time the trust becomes effective, plus twenty-one years and nine months. As long as the named persons are living, or within twenty-one years and nine months after their deaths, persons who had not been born when the trust was set up could be beneficiaries under the trust agreement. This usually applies to grandchildren born after a trust is created.

In one often-cited case, the courts upheld the validity of a trust created in 1926 to continue until twenty-one years and nine months after the death of all lineal descendants of Queen Victoria who were then living. There were 120 lineal descendants of the Queen at that time.

After the maximum period expires, the trust is terminated and the property is distributed in the fashion set forth in the agreement.

Experts suggest that you review the trust agreement periodically and update it as often as necessary—if the revisions can be made legally. They cite this case history to show why it can be important:

A wealthy New York woman established a testamentary trust in her will, naming her husband, a friend, and two sisters as beneficiaries. But she didn't specify what to do with the shares of any beneficiary who died before she did. Three of the four beneficiaries did die first, and the courts had to decide whether the remainder of the trust should be distributed as if she died intestate or should go to the surviving beneficiary.

Joint ownership

Although trusts are becoming more popular as an estate planning tool, they still are not nearly as common as joint ownership, another way to pass along property without involving it in the probate process.

Joint ownership is favored by many persons, particularly married couples, because of its simplicity.

An example: When a home is held in the names of husband and wife, the property goes automatically, on the death of one owner, to the survivor. The transfer is unaffected by the deceased person's will. This can save executor's fees, other administrative costs and, perhaps most important, it can avoid the often time-consuming probate procedure.

In addition to the family home, almost any type of property can be jointly owned—including stocks, bonds, other real estate, and bank accounts. You should keep in mind that there are three distinct types of joint ownership. They are:

Joint tenancy: All of the property passes to the survivor on the death of one. While both owners are living, either can usually break up ownership even against the will of the other joint owner.

Tenancy by entirety: This form can be used only by le-

gally married persons. The entire property goes to the survivor on the death of one. But while both are living, neither can sell the property without approval of the other.

Tenancy in common: Each owns an undivided interest in
the property, and each may sell his own portion. Upon
death of one, his portion of the property does not automatically go to the other. Instead, it goes to the heirs of the
owner who died.

The first two types—joint tenancy and tenancy by entirety—are by far the most common. Their usage has, in some
instances, become almost customary. The deeds to 85 percent of the private homes in one western state were made
out in the names of husband and wife in joint tenancy.

Many married couples jointly hold common stocks. The
stock would be registered something like this: "John Smith
and Mary Smith, as joint tenants with right of survivorship, and not as tenants in common." When stock is registered in this manner, it automatically passes to the survivor upon the death of one. Jointly held stock also has a tax
advantage that appeals to many married couples. On such
stock, the first $200 in dividends is exempt from income
taxes, compared with the $100 exemption on individually
owned stock.

U.S. Savings Bonds also are commonly held jointly. If a
bond is registered "John Smith or Mary Smith," the survivor automatically becomes the sole owner. Savings bonds
also can be registered this way: "John Smith P.O.D. Mary
Smith." The initials P.O.D. stand for "payable on death."
This isn't joint ownership. John is the sole owner while he
lives. But if he dies first, the net result is the same as joint
ownership. Mary becomes the owner of the bond.

Another tax advantage: Joint ownership of property permits the splitting of income or gains. This would benefit
married couples only if they file separate tax returns, instead of a joint return.

In addition, income realized from real estate jointly owned by a married couple may be split between husband and wife without gift tax liability. If the property were owned by one spouse, who transferred the income to the other, then the excess over $6,000 a year would be subject to gift tax.

Because of its widespread usage and the fact that the transfer of property occurs automatically upon death of one partner, the joint ownership arrangement often is referred to as the "poor man's will." Unless a man has considerable wealth, he probably can safely pass along some property by joint ownership.

But estate planners caution that joint ownership is not a substitute for a will. In fact, they say, thoughtless use of a joint tenancy form sometimes can have the effect of defeating a person's will. One attorney cited this example:

A widower specified in his will that he wanted the family home to go to his three sons. He later remarried and placed the deed to the home in joint tenancy with his second wife. When he died, the second wife became sole owner as surviving joint tenant—despite the provision in the will that the three sons were to get the home. The second wife never got along with her stepsons, and when she died a few years later her will left the home to her sister. The sons never got the family home.

Similar problems can be encountered if both owners under a joint tenancy arrangement die in a common accident or in quick succession.

As a general rule, there is no particular estate tax advantage to joint ownership, and there could be disadvantages. When a co-owner dies, the total value of jointly owned property would be included in his estate for tax purposes, just as if he had owned it alone. But if the survivor could prove that he or she contributed to the purchase price, then the part represented by this contribution would be excluded. The total value of the property again may be subject to estate taxation when the surviving co-owner dies.

There are special tax rules for jointly-held property received through inheritance. These and other estate tax provisions are complex, and state laws governing estate taxes can vary, so authorities say it usually is wise to consult an attorney, perhaps a tax attorney, before deciding whether joint ownership is best for you. In many instances, the advantages of joint ownership would outweigh the disadvantages. Even if they don't, the specialists you consult may be able to suggest substitute legal devices that would achieve the desired results yet avoid possible pitfalls of joint ownership.

For example, if the right of the survivor to receive the property automatically is the chief attraction of joint ownership, experts suggest that a revocable trust could achieve the same result. Such a trust would assure that the property would go to the named beneficiary, while avoiding the costs and delay of estate administration and the publicity of will probate. The person setting up the trust could maintain control of the property during his lifetime and could change the trust arrangement if necessary.

Life insurance

Life insurance is another asset that passes directly to a named beneficiary without the necessity of being mentioned in a will or going through the probate process. For many individuals of modest means, the proceeds of life insurance policies make up the largest single item of the estate they leave for their survivors.

The proceeds of a life insurance policy usually must be included in computing the amount of an estate for estate tax purposes. There are exceptions. One way to skirt this estate tax liability is to surrender all rights to the policy during your lifetime. A man, for example, might give life insurance policies outright to his wife or his children. If he surrenders all "rights of ownership" in the policies—including the right to borrow on them or to change beneficiaries—they are not considered part of his estate and thus escape estate taxes. Remember, though, that if a man turns over insurance policies on his life to his wife, and she dies first, the cash value of the policies will be part of her estate for tax purposes.

Estate planners point out another hazard: Suppose a man has given a $50,000 life insurance policy to his wife. She is the sole owner. Then there is a family disagreement and the wife and husband separate. The husband may wish he had held on to that policy so he could make someone else the beneficiary.

Annuity contracts can also bypass the probate process so long as your estate is not named as beneficiary. The same is true of qualified employee benefit plans, such as profit-sharing, deferred compensation, and pensions.

Having passed the perils of probate, an estate still faces another formidable problem—taxes. It is the subject of the next and concluding chapter.

12
Cutting Down on Taxes

"Anyone may so arrange his affairs that his taxes shall be as low as possible; he is not bound to choose that pattern which will best pay the Treasury; there is not even a patriotic duty to increase one's taxes."

This was written many years ago by Judge Learned Hand. The famed jurist's words are just as valid today, when the government itself has provided ways to lighten the tax burden it imposes.

By taking advantage of available tax shelters, you can sharply reduce—perhaps even eliminate entirely—the bite taxes will take from your estate. Proper planning is the key.

Anyone who tries to evade taxes is courting trouble. This chapter outlines different ways you can cut tax costs through acceptable and legitimate methods.

We are concerned principally with the federal estate tax and the federal gift tax. States also impose what are known variously as "estate," "inheritance," or "succession" taxes. These vary widely, but on the whole, state taxes are small compared with those of the federal government. As a general rule, they may be allowed as a credit against the federal tax.

If your estate is of modest size, it may be completely free of tax. A new federal estate and gift tax, enacted in 1976, provides a special individual credit that in effect exempts from tax estates up to $120,667 in value. If the death occurred in 1977, this exempt amount is even higher. It increases year by year until 1981, when, the exempt amount reaches $175,625. The new tax credit replaced the old, less generous $60,000 exemption.

There are two additional devices in the new law which allow somewhat larger estates to escape tax completely.

The first is the marital deduction, which exempts from tax $250,000 or one-half of the total estate—whichever is larger—if the amount is bequeathed to a spouse. Thus, combining the marital deduction and the personal credit, you could exempt up to $370,667 from·tax.

The second device is the special valuation of a family farm or business, which allows you to reduce the amount of your estate by up to $500,000 under certain circumstances. We will explain that later.

The federal estate tax is steeply graduated. It starts at 30 percent and runs to a peak rate of 70 percent for "taxable" estates in excess of $5 million.

The "taxable" estate is the gross estate less the marital deduction, if any, and deductions for debts, expenses, and charitable contributions. The new credit also, in effect, reduces the amount of the taxable estate, although for technical reasons it is deducted from the amount of tax that would otherwise be owed rather than from the size of the estate.

Estate and Gift Tax Rates

If the tentative tax is computed on an amount that is:	The tentative tax is:
Not over $10,000	18% of the amount
Over $10,000 but not over $20,000	$1,800, plus 20% of the amount over $10,000
Over $20,000 but not over $40,000	$3,800, plus 22% of the amount over $20,000
Over $40,000 but not over $60,000	$8,200, plus 24% of the amount over $40,000
Over $60,000 but not over $80,000	$13,000, plus 26% of the amount over $60,000
Over $80,000 but not over $100,000	$18,200, plus 28% of the amount over $80,000
Over $100,000 but not over $150,000	$23,800, plus 30% of the amount over $100,000
Over $150,000 but not over $250,000	$38,800, plus 32% of the amount over $150,000
Over $250,000 but not over $500,000	$70,800, plus 34% of the amount over $250,000
Over $500,000 but not over $750,000	$155,800, plus 37% of the amount over $500,000
Over $750,000 but not over $1,000,000	$248,300, plus 39% of the amount over $750,000
Over $1,000,000 but not over $1,250,000	$345,000, plus 41% of the amount over $1,000,000
Over $1,250,000 but not over $1,500,000	$448,300, plus 43% of the amount over $1,250,000
Over $1,500,000 but not over $2,000,000	$555,800, plus 45% of the amount over $1,500,000
Over $2,000,000 but not over $2,500,000	$780,800, plus 49% of the amount over $2,000,000
Over $2,500,000 but not over $3,000,000	$1,025,800, plus 53% of the amount over $2,500,000
Over $3,000,000 but not over $3,500,000	$1,290,800, plus 57% of the amount over $3,000,000
Over $3,500,000 but not over $4,000,000	$1,575,800, plus 61% of the amount over $3,500,000
Over $4,000,000 but not over $4,500,000	$1,880,800, plus 65% of the amount over $4,000,000
Over $4,500,000 but not over $5,000,000	$2,205,800, plus 69% of the amount over $4,500,000
Over $5,000,000	$2,550,800, plus 70% of the amount over $5,000,000

All of your property—real and personal, tangible, and intangible—make up your gross estate. That means your house and its contents, your automobile, cash, bank and savings accounts, stocks and bonds, business interests, and a wide range of other belongings such as the books in your library, the tools in your workshop, and the equipment in your home darkroom.

It includes the following types of property:

• *Life insurance:* Proceeds of life insurance policies sometimes are subject to the estate tax. This is when (1) death benefits are made payable to the estate or (2) when a beneficiary is named and you, the insured, retain what is known as "incidents of ownership" in the policy. The general rule is that if you retain the right to make any change in the policy this is considered to be an "incident of ownership." Examples would be if you retain the right to change the beneficiary, to make loans against its cash value, to receive dividends, or to select settlement options. If, however, you give the policy to another person and surrender all rights to make changes in it, then it would not be included in your gross estate and would not be subject to estate taxes.

• *Jointly owned property:* Although jointly owned property passes to the survivor without going through a will or the probate process, it nevertheless is subject to federal estate taxes to the extent that the person whose estate is involved contributed to the purchase price. The government assumes for estate tax purposes that the first joint owner to die contributed the entire purchase price, in the case of real estate or other property, or the entire amount of money in a joint checking or savings account. If the survivor put up any of the money, then the burden is on him —or her—to prove it. An illustration of how this works:

Mr. and Mrs. Smith owned their home jointly. Mrs. Smith was a housewife and did not contribute any money toward the purchase price of the home. But if Mrs. Smith dies first, the government will assume she put up all the money, and it will be up to Mr. Smith to prove otherwise to the satisfaction of the taxing authorities.

• *Trusts:* The property in a revocable lifetime trust is subject to federal estate taxes when the person who set up the trust dies. Testamentary trusts—those established by a will—also are subject to the estate tax. Property in an irrevocable lifetime trust may be taxed, too, if the person who set up the trust gets some benefit from it or if he can alter any of the terms of the trust.

Exemptions and deductions

Funeral costs are subtracted from your estate before estate taxes are calculated. So are all expenses related to the administration of your estate. Examples of these expenses are executors' commissions and attorneys' fees. Before you figure the tax bill, you also can deduct from your gross estate all of your debts—outstanding loans, a home mortgage, unpaid taxes, and whatever else you may owe.

When you subtract these deductions from your gross estate, you have a new figure—your adjusted gross estate. Charitable gifts may be deducted from this figure. The amount of your adjusted gross estate is used to calculate perhaps the most valuable deduction of all—that of the marital deduction.

The marital deduction

This allows a widow or widower to inherit tax-free half of a spouse's adjusted gross estate. Such a deduction can take much of the sting out of estate taxes. An estate planner calls the marital deduction "easily the most valuaable tool available for alleviating estate tax erosion."

Before 1948, tax benefits under the marital deduction were available only in the community property states—Cal-

Taxes on Your Estate After Bequests to Your Wife

A. On a $200,000 estate:

When wife receives:	Amount of tax:
Entire estate	$ 0
Half of estate	$ 0
Third of estate	$ 3,800
None of estate	$ 24,800

B. On a $300,000 estate:

When wife receives:	Amount of tax:
Entire estate	$ 0
Half of estate	$ 8,800
Third of estate	$ 24,800
None of estate	$ 57,800

C. On a $500,000 estate:

When wife receives:	Amount of tax:
Entire estate	$ 40,800
Half of estate	$ 40,800
Third of estate	$ 69,133
None of estate	$125,800

D. On a $1,000,000 estate:

When wife receives:	Amount of tax:
Entire estate	$125,800
Half of estate	$125,800
Third of estate	$187,467
None of estate	$315,800

Note: Figures based on assumption that husband owns entire estate, and dies first.

ifornia, Arizona, Nevada, New Mexico, Idaho, Texas, Louisiana, and Washington. In these states, each spouse owns half of all property earned and accumulated by either husband or wife during marriage.

Thus, when one partner dies, only half of the community property is subject to estate taxes. Prior to 1948, if a man living in a non-community property state left property to his wife, it was all subject to estate taxes upon his death. If this property remained in her estate until she died, when it passed on to her beneficiaries it was taxed a second time.

The marital deduction was enacted to equalize the tax situation between common law and community property states. Under it, if at least half the estate is left to the surviving spouse, only one-half of the total estate is taxable when the first mate dies.

In this example, George Jones examined three ways of distributing an estate of $700,000.

1. Instead of passing property to his wife, he could give it directly to his children. The marital deduction could not be used, and federal and state estate taxes would total $199,800.

2. He could leave his entire estate to his wife. One-half of the estate, or $350,000, qualifies for the marital deduction. After the personal credit, the estate taxes would total $74,800. In the event she dies more than ten years later, assuming the entire $625,200 bequest remains intact and she does not remarry, her estate is subject to taxes of $155,124. Add this to the $74,800 paid at the time of her husband's death and the combined estate taxes come to $229,924.

3. He could take full advantage of the marital deduction and leave his wife only half of the estate, his children the other half. No taxes are due on the wife's portion, but taxes of $74,800 are due on the other half. Again assuming his wife died ten years later without remarrying, the $350,000 she had received from her husband could pass to the children

with payment of another $57,800 in taxes. The combined taxes would be $132,600. In this case, use of the marital deduction would save his estate $97,324.

Estate planners offer this word of caution: The marital deduction is not automatic. You must know what type of property transfers qualify.

Two requirements must be met to qualify for the marital deduction. First, the property must actually pass to the surviving spouse. Second, the transfer must be made under conditions which insure that it will be included in her taxable estate when she dies—if she still has it.

Property does not have to be included in your will to qualify for the marital deduction. It can pass outside your will—just so long as it is included in your gross estate. For example, insurance proceeds payable to your wife which are part of your gross estate can qualify. So can joint property which she takes by right of survivorship, if it is included in your gross estate.

Trusts can qualify for the marital exemption too, but the process is a bit more complicated. One general rule is this: If you want to obtain the benefits of the deduction, you must give your wife certain control over the trust property. You cannot, for example, simply give her the income from a trust and still receive the deduction.

Before a trust arrangement can qualify for the marital deduction, it must meet specific requirements set forth in the tax law. One requirement is that the principal of the trust—the money or property that is placed in the trust—must pass to the wife's estate at her death and thus be subject to estate taxes.

Estate planners say that unless there are compelling nontax reasons against leaving your spouse one-half of your estate, it usually is wise to take full advantage of the marital deduction. For instance, suppose you have an estate of $900,000. If you leave your wife half, the federal estate tax will be $108,800. If you don't, your estate taxes will be $276,800—a difference of $168,000.

Sometimes, it may *not* be wise to use the marital deduction. An example is when the husband and wife have estates that are about the same size. Use of the marital deduction will reduce the tax bite on the husband's estate, assuming he dies first. But his property is added to his wife's estate, so that when she dies, her taxes will be greatly increased. It is possible that in such a case the combined taxes on both estates would be larger than if the husband had not used the marital deduction.

For the maximum in tax savings, estate planners say it generally is best to limit the bequest to your spouse to exactly 50 percent of your gross estate. There are no tax savings realized on the sum in excess of 50 percent. On the contrary, there may be unnecessary double taxation. The amount above 50 percent will be taxed first in your estate, then in hers.

What happens when the husband and wife die simultaneously in a common accident? Is the marital deduction available in such cases?

The answer would appear to be "no," since the laws of most states specify that in such simultaneous deaths, each spouse is presumed to survive the other. Neither inherits from the other; thus no marital deduction.

But it is possible to change this presumption. This can be done by inserting into the will, trust, or insurance contract a provision stating that in the event of simultaneous deaths in a common accident, one spouse is presumed to have survived the other. Such a provision is especially advisable when one spouse, say the wife, has little or no property, and the husband has a substantial amount. Here's why:

Suppose a man has a $500,000 estate and intends to leave half of it to his wife, who has no property of her own. If they were to die simultaneously in an automobile or other accident, under the laws of their state the husband would be presumed to have survived his wife. She would inherit none of his estate. There would be no marital deduction. The federal estates taxes would be $125,800. But if the husband were to insert into his will a provision stating that in case both died in a common accident it was to be presumed that she survived, then half of his estate could pass to her. Thus, for tax purposes, each of them would have an estate of $250,000. The tax on each estate would be $40,800, for a combined tax of $81,600—a tax savings of $44,200.

Federal estate tax regulations include provisions designed to prevent the same property from being taxed twice within a relatively short period. Here's how this works:

Assume that John Smith leaves all his property to his brother, Sam. If Sam's death occurs within ten years of his brother's, his estate is allowed a tax credit for the tax paid at John's death, as follows: 100 percent of the tax if he dies within two years; 80 percent, if he dies within three or four years; 60 percent, if he dies within five or six years; 40 percent, if he dies within seven or eight years; 20 percent, if he dies within nine or ten years. If Sam survives his brother by more than ten years, there would be no offset of the earlier tax.

The tax credit applies only to property passing outside the marital deduction.

Your generosity can help reduce the estate tax bite. There are two possibilities:

1. You can specify in your will that certain charitable contributions be made from your estate. These contributions are deducted from the estate before any taxes are calculated.

2. You can give away some of your assets during your lifetime, reducing the size of your estate and thus cutting down on estate taxes.

Three Ways to Pass an Estate

1. Husband leaves whole estate to wife, who then leaves it to children at her death

Husband's Estate *	Estate Tax
Up to $120,000	$0
$150,000	$0
$200,000	$7,800
$300,000	$40,800
$500,000	$135,728
$1,000,000	$375,538
$2,000,000	$706,306

2. Husband leaves entire estate to the children

Husband's Estate *	Estate Tax
Up to $120,000	$0
$150,000	$8,800
$200,000	$24,800
$300,000	$57,800
$500,000	$125,800
$1,000,000	$315,800
$2,000,000	$750,800

3. Husband leaves half to wife, half to children—wife then leaves her half to children

Husband's Estate *	Estate Tax
Up to $120,000	$0
$150,000	$0
$200,000	$0
$300,000	$4,300
$500,000	$51,544
$1,000,000	$191,828
$2,000,000	$492,754

Note: Figures assume the wife preserves her share of the estate and lives at least 10 years longer than her husband. They cover the total estate taxes—the husband's plus the wife's at her death.

*After tax deductions for expenses of the estate, bequests to charity, etc.

Before you make a charitable bequest in your will, make certain that the gift qualifies for a deduction under the federal estate tax law. The tax law specifies that deductions will be allowed for gifts to groups operated exclusively for religious, charitable, scientific, literary, or educational purposes, if the group does not devote a substantial part of its activity to carrying on propaganda or attempting to influence legislation.

Contributions to organizations such as the Red Cross, the Boy Scouts, the Salvation Army, and other well-known charitable organizations clearly qualify for the deduction. So do most gifts to churches, universities, and hospitals.

Gifts also qualify if they go to the United States Government, or any state or political subdivision and are used exclusively for "public purposes." For example, if you leave property to your city with instructions that it be used for a community park, the value of the land could be deducted from your estate.

If you want to avoid estate taxes completely, one way to do it would be to give your entire estate to charity. The income tax law limits the deduction you can take for charitable contributions, but you can give your whole estate to charity without paying taxes.

Andrew Mellon left almost his entire estate of about $100 million to the A. W. Mellon Educational and Charitable Trust, thus avoiding estate taxes of about $67 million.

When Henry Ford died in 1947, he owned about 1,900,000 shares of stock in the Ford Motor Company. He left 1,805,000 shares of non-voting stock to the Ford Foundation—tax-free. The remaining shares of voting stock were left to his heirs.

A relatively wealthy individual can reduce his estate taxes through charitable contributions while providing income for his family. This is done by establishing a charitable trust. Income from the trust goes to a designated beneficiary for life, with the principal going to charity. Here's an example of how a charitable trust can work:

John Adams, a widower, has an estate of $250,000 which he wants to leave in a way that will provide first for the security of his daughter, and then will result in a contribution to his favorite charity. If he leaves it all to his daughter, with the understanding that it eventually will go to his favorite charity, estate taxes will total $40,800, and his daughter would have $209,200. Assuming an annual return of 6 percent, this amount would provide yearly income of $12,552 for his daughter.

Some wealthy persons use life insurance to give to charity and at the same time to reduce estate taxes. One authority gave this example:

A business executive with an estate of $1 million purchased a $500,000 life insurance policy and named his church as irrevocable beneficiary of the policy. He retained an "incident of ownership," such as the right to specify the settlement option by which the beneficiary would receive the proceeds. Retention of this "incident of ownership" means the policy proceeds would be included in his total estate, increasing it from $1 million to $1.5 million.

Upon his death, his wife could receive one-half of the total or $750,000, tax-free under the marital deduction. The $500,000 for the church would be deducted from the remaining $750,000, leaving $250,000. After use of the personal credit, total estate taxes would be $40,800.

If he had not purchased the insurance policy his estate would have totaled $1 million, half of which could have gone to his wife tax-free under the marital deduction. This would have left $500,000. After use of the personal credit, his estate taxes would be $125,800—or $85,000 more than under the other estate plan.

Family farm or business

If you own and operate a farm or business and want to

bequeath it to a member of your family, you may be able to reduce by up to $500,000 the valuation of that property for estate tax purposes. In the past, such properties had to be valued at their "highest and best use"—that is, farmland in the vicinity of a spreading suburb was assessed by the Internal Revenue Service at the price it would bring from real estate developers eager to subdivide it. The 1976 law allows the value of such property to be calculated for estate tax purposes on its worth as farm or business property, provided certain conditions are met.

Among the conditions are that the farm or business must amount to at least 50 percent of the decedent's gross estate; it must be willed to a member of the decedent's family (children, spouse, grandchildren, aunts or uncles, or their children or grandchildren); and members of the family must have owned and worked in the farm or business for at least five of the eight preceding years.

Consider the case of Farmer Brown, who leaves his 1,000-acre farm to his son. Apart from the farm, the estate is worth only $50,000. Farmers are willing to pay $120 an acre for land in this region, but a real estate developer recently paid $600 an acre for a parcel of farmland to build a shopping center not far away. Valued on this basis, the farm would be worth $600,000, and the estate tax would be $181,300. But using the special valuation, Farmer Brown's executor could have the farm assessed at $120,000, lowering the total value of the estate to $170,000 and reducing the tax bite to $15,200—a whopping difference of $166,100.

In the face of death

Ideally, estate planning should be reviewed throughout a person's mature years to ensure a favorable settlement for one's survivors. However, it is often the case that as a person nears old age or becomes terminally ill, he becomes more concerned about the financial provisions he has made for his dependents. When this anxiety arises, it can be reduced by making use of a provision in the law governing estate taxes.

This provision of the law allows the use of certain Treasury bonds to pay federal estate taxes. Because these bonds pay lower interest rates than high-grade corporate bonds, they can be purchased on the open market for substantially less than face value. However, they can be used at face value for the purpose of paying federal estate taxes. Considerable savings can be realized because of this difference between purchase cost and face value.

If this use of Treasury bonds is contemplated, certain requirements must be met: the deceased person must have owned the bonds at the time of his death; they must be included in his estate; and they must be redeemed to pay estate taxes before they mature or prior to the date the Treasury Department may call for their redemption before maturity.

If the bonds are jointly owned, that part which was the property of the deceased and was included in his estate can be used to pay estate taxes. Special rules apply if the bonds are part of a trust; professional guidance should be sought in such a case.

Because of the bonds' relatively low rate of interest, some financial advisers do not recommend their purchase if a person anticipates many more years of life. Tax-free bonds or bonds with higher rates of interest are often recommended instead.

However, you should consider two points. First, the low interest rate is what makes these Treasury bonds available on the open market at a discount. The lower purchase price should be included when calculating the effective yield of these bonds.

And second, these bonds would serve as a sort of life insurance policy to help pay federal taxes on your estate should you die accidentally.

Treasury Bonds Redeemable at Face Value In the Payment of Federal Estate Taxes

Issue & Interest	Payable on (If not previously recalled)	Redeemable on call on and after	Nov. 5, 1976 asked price ($1,000 bond)
1978–83 (3¼)	June 15, 1983	June 15, 1978	$844.38
1980 (4)	February 15, 1980	—	937.50
1980 (3½)	November 15, 1980	—	910.63
1985 (3¼)	May 15, 1985	—	849.38
1987–92 (4¼)	August 15, 1992	August 15, 1987	859.38
1988–93 (4)	February 15, 1993	February 15, 1988	860.63
1989–94 (4⅛)	May 15, 1994	May 15, 1989	853.13
1990 (3½)	February 15, 1990	—	849.38
1995 (3)	February 15, 1995	—	848.75
1998 (3½)	November 15, 1998	—	848.75

Lifetime giving

Perhaps the simplest way to reduce your estate taxes is to give away some of your property during your lifetime. This reduces the size of your estate and thus reduces the amount of taxes due.

Of course, if your gifts are large enough, they will become subject to the gift tax, and the 1976 tax law raised gift tax rates so that they equal estate tax rates. The gift tax rates formerly were 25 percent of the estate tax rates. In addition, the new law eliminated the old $30,000 lifetime exemption from the gift tax.

Nevertheless, there are still some important deductions

234 PLANNING YOUR FINANCIAL FUTURE

and exclusions under the gift tax laws that allow people to give away substantial sums during their lifetime without incurring any gift tax liability.

Every year, for example, you can give up to $3,000 each to as many persons as you wish without paying any gift tax. While this does not affect the income taxes you must pay, you are reducing the amount of your assets that eventually will become subject to the estate tax.

Suppose you have five children and ten grandchildren. Each year you can give each of them $3,000. In five years your tax-free gifts would total $225,000.

In addition, the new law established a $100,000 lifetime exemption from the gift tax for amounts given to a spouse. When combined with the $250,000 marital deduction for estate taxes and the personal estate tax credit, this provision can make it possible for a man to pass nearly $500,000 in assets to his wife free of estate or gift taxes.

Under some circumstances, however, claims under the gift tax marital deduction can reduce the marital deduction under the estate tax. You should consult a lawyer or other qualified estate adviser before going through with such a plan.

Another rule to remember is that all gifts in excess of the $3,000 exemptions made in the last three years before death are in effect revoked, and the amounts included in the taxable estate. This is to prevent "deathbed" transfers aimed at reducing the estate tax.

Except for donations to charitable, educational, and religious organizations, gifts cannot be taken as deductions against income taxes. The gift tax is paid by the person who makes the gift—the donor—and not by the person who receives it. But the government has the right to collect from the recipient if the donor does not pay the tax.

Besides the federal tax, gift taxes have been enacted by a number of states. You should check with your lawyer to determine whether state taxes might apply to you. Gen-

How the Personal Exemption Works

Assume an estate of $300,000. First you calculate a "tentative tax" from the new tax rate schedule: $87,800. Then you deduct from that the amount of the personal credit: $30,000. This leaves an estate tax due of $57,800. The same tax rate and credit schedules apply to the gift tax, but the credit can be used only once. It cannot be deducted from both the tentative gift tax due and the tentative estate tax. The amount of the credit rises in future as follows:

Year	Amount of Credit	Amount of Estate Exempt from Tax
1977	$30,000	$120,667
1978	$34,000	$134,000
1979	$38,000	$147,333
1980	$42,500	$161,563
1981 and after	$47,000	$175,625

Source: U.S. House of Representatives Committee on Ways and Means

erally, state taxes are low as compared with the federal gift tax, but they cannot be deducted or used as a credit in figuring the federal gift tax.

People sometimes attempt to escape the gift tax by a more or less fictitious sale of property. You might, for example, sell your brother a vacant lot for $100. But if the government determines by expert appraisal or assessed value that the lot was worth $1,000, it will consider the transaction as a gift of $900 on your part.

The same is true in the sale of securities. If you sold your son 100 shares of XYZ Corporation for $10 a share, or a total of $1,000, when the same stock was selling in the open market at $15 a share, or $1,500 for 100 shares, then you would be making a gift of $500.

What happens when you buy property with your own

money, but put the title into a form of joint ownership? Is a gift tax due?

As a general rule, a gift tax is due on one-half of the value of the property. If, for example, you purchased a house and put the title in the names of both your daughter and yourself, then you would have made a gift to her of one-half of the value of the house.

There is one important exception. If a husband buys property and puts it in the name of himself and his wife as joint owners, no gift is deemed to have taken place. But there is a gift at the time the property is sold if a spouse receives more from the sale than the proportionate share contributed to the original purchase price. For example, Edward Brown, with his own money, buys a farm for $50,000 and places the title in his and his wife's name as joint owners. No gift tax is due. But if he later sells the farm and turns the money he receives over to his wife, then a gift tax is due since the wife did not contribute toward the purchase price.

In conclusion, here are some do's and don't's in planning your estate:

Things to do:

• Draw a will and keep it up to date. Make sure your wife does the same.

• Consider the advantages of giving away property during your lifetime, rather than letting it all accumulate in your estate.

• Look into trusts as a way to accomplish special purposes and avoid some delays of probate.

• Make sure that your estate plan provides guardianship and financial and investment guidance for minor children in your family, or for any others who may be incompetent to manage for themselves.

• Review your whole estate plan once a year.

• Keep your plan flexible to allow for changes in your financial position and your family situation.

• Get expert legal advice.

Things not to do:

• Don't call on a friend or neighbor to be executor of your estate if you have a substantial amount of property. Best bet: A bank, trust company, or other specialist in financial management.

• Don't take it for granted that your property will go automatically to those you want to have it, unless you have an airtight will.

• Don't assume your estate is "too small to worry about." Even small amounts of property should be disposed of carefully. Many people today find their estates are larger than they realized.

• Don't put off drawing a will and making an estate plan.

• Don't try to economize in planning your estate. Get the best help you can afford.

Glossary of Words and Phrases Related to Investments, Insurance, Wills

ACTUARY—A person professionally trained in the technical aspects of insurance, particularly in the mathematics of mortality tables and the calculation of premiums, reserves, and other values.

ADMINISTRATOR—The person appointed by a court to settle an estate, usually when there is no will.

ANNUAL REPORT—The financial statement issued annually by a corporation to its stockholders.

ASSETS—Everything a corporation owns, including cash, investments, accounts due, materials and inventories, buildings and machinery.

ASSIGNMENT—The legal transfer of rights or interests in property to another person.

AUTOMATIC PREMIUM LOAN—A provision in a life insurance policy authorizing the company to pay automatically by means of a policy loan any premium not paid by the end of the grace period.

AVERAGE—A way of measuring the trend of prices on the stock exchanges.

BEAR—Someone who believes the stock market will decline.

BEAR MARKET—A declining market.

BENEFICIARY—A person named in an insurance policy or a will to receive property.

BEQUEATH—The legal word used to apply to the giving of property by will.

BID AND ASKED—The bid is the highest price anyone is willing to pay for a security at a given time; the *asked* is the lowest price anyone will take at that time.

BIG BOARD—A popular name for the New York Stock Exchange.

BLUE CHIP—Common stock in a nationally known company with a proven ability to make money and pay dividends in good times and bad.

BOND—A certificate issued as evidence of a debt incurred by a corporation.

BROKER—An agent who handles the public's orders to buy and sell securities.

BULL—One who believes the stock market will rise.

BULL MARKET—A rising market.

CAPITAL GAIN or CAPITAL LOSS—The profit or loss from the sale of capital assets.

CASH or SURRENDER VALUE—The amount available in cash upon voluntary termination of an insurance policy before it becomes payable by death or maturity.

CODICIL—A document, executed with all the formality of a will, used to amend the provisions of an existing will.

COMMON STOCK—Securities that represent an ownership interest in a corporation.

CONVERTIBLE—A bond or preferred share that may be exchanged for common stock of the same company.

CONVERTIBLE TERM INSURANCE—Term insurance which can

be exchanged without taking a medical examination for another insurance plan.

CREDIT LIFE INSURANCE—Term life insurance issued through a lender or lending agency to cover payment of a loan, installment purchase, or other personal debt in case of death.

CUMULATIVE PREFERRED—A stock having a provision that if one or more dividends are omitted, the omitted dividends must be paid before any dividends may be paid on the company's common stock.

DEALER—An individual or a firm in the securities business acting as a principal rather than as an agent.

DISABILITY BENEFIT—A provision added to a life insurance policy for waiver of premium, and sometimes payment of monthly income, if the insured becomes permanently and totally disabled.

DIVERSIFICATION—Spreading investments among different companies in different fields.

DIVIDEND—The payment designated by a corporation to be distributed pro rata among outstanding shares of stock.

DOLLAR COST AVERAGING—A method of purchasing securities at regular intervals with a fixed amount of dollars, regardless of the prevailing prices of the securities.

DOUBLE INDEMNITY—A death benefit providing for additional payment in an amount equal to the face value of a policy in case of death by accident.

ENDOWMENT INSURANCE—Insurance payable to the insured on a maturity date stated in the policy, or to a beneficiary if the insured dies prior to that date.

ESTATE—All property, real and personal, tangible and intangible, in which a person has an interest.

EX-DIVIDEND—A synonym for "without dividend." The buyer of a stock "ex-dividend" does not receive declared dividends.

EXECUTOR—The person named in a will to carry out its terms. When it is a woman, the word "executrix" is used.

FACE VALUE—The value that appears on the front of a bond or insurance policy; usually the amount the issuing company promises to pay at maturity.

FAMILY POLICY—A life insurance policy providing insurance on all or several family members in one contract.

GROUP LIFE INSURANCE—Life insurance issued, usually without medical examination, on a group of persons under a single master policy.

GUARDIAN—A person appointed to protect the interests of a minor.

HOLOGRAPHIC WILL—A will written by the testator in his own handwriting.

INDENTURE—A written agreement under which bonds are issued, specifying the maturity date, interest rate, security, and other terms.

INDUSTRIAL LIFE INSURANCE—Life insurance issued in small amounts, usually less than $1,000, with premiums payable on a weekly or monthly basis. The premiums generally are collected at the home by an insurance agent.

INSURABILITY—Acceptability to the company of an applicant for life insurance.

INTEREST—Payments a borrower pays a lender for the use of his money.

INTESTACY or INTESTATE—Dying without a will.

INVESTMENT—The use of money for the purpose of making more money—to gain income, increase capital, or both.

INVESTMENT COUNSELOR—One who provides investment advisory and supervisory services.

JOINT TENANTS—Persons who own an equal interest in the same property, all of which passes to the survivor.

JOINT WILL—A will that is drawn and executed by more than one person with the intention that it be the will of each of them.

LAPSED POLICY—A policy terminated for nonpayment of premiums. The term is sometimes limited to a termination occurring before the policy has a cash value.

LEGACY—A provision in a will which leaves certain personal property to a named individual. It is also known as a bequest.

LEGATEE—A person who is given personal property under a will.

LETTERS OF ADMINISTRATION—Documents usually issued by a probate court giving an administrator the authority to administer the estate of the person who made the will.

LETTERS TESTAMENTARY—Documents issued by a probate court giving a person named as executor in a will the authority to administer the estate of the person who made the will.

LEVEL PREMIUM INSURANCE—Insurance for which the cost is distributed evenly over the period during which premiums are paid.

LIFE EXPECTANCY—The average number of years of life remaining for persons of a given age.

LIFE TENANTS—Persons who receive income from a trust during their lives; they are also known as income beneficiaries.

LIVING TRUST—A type of trust that goes into effect during the life of the person who creates the trust.

LOAD—The portion of the price of mutual fund shares that covers sales commissions and other distribution costs.

MARGIN—The amount paid by a customer when he uses credit to buy a security. For example, when a 70 percent margin requirement is in force, the buyer must put up 70 percent cash when he buys a stock.

MARKET ORDER—An order by a customer to a broker to buy or sell at the best price available when the order reaches the trading floor.

MARKET PRICE—In the case of a stock, market price usually is considered the last reported price at which the stock is sold.

MATURITY—The date on which a loan or bond comes due and is to be paid off.

MONTHLY INVESTMENT PLAN—A method of buying New York Stock Exchange listed shares on a regular payment plan.

MORTGAGE BOND—A bond secured by a mortgage on a stated piece of property.

MUNICIPAL BOND—A bond issued by a state or political subdivision, such as a county, city, or town; or issued by state agencies and authorities.

MUTUAL LIFE INSURANCE COMPANY—A life insurance company without stockholders, whose management is directed by a board elected by the policyholders.

MUTUAL WILLS—Separate documents executed by two persons, usually husband and wife, containing reciprocal provisions for the disposition of their property.

NON-CUMULATIVE—Refers to a preferred stock on which unpaid dividends do not accumulate.

NONCUPATIVE WILL—An oral will by which a person disposes of his property in the event of his death. In many states, courts refuse to accept noncupative wills.

NONFORFEITURE OPTION—One of the choices available to the policyholder if he discontinues the required premium payments. The policy value, if any, may be taken in cash, as extended term insurance, or as reduced paid-up life insurance.

NONPARTICIPATING INSURANCE—Insurance on which the premium is calculated to cover as closely as possible the anticipated cost of the insurance protection and on which no dividends are payable.

ODD LOT—An amount of stock less than the established 100-share unit of trading.

OFFER—The price at which a person will sell a security.

OVER-THE-COUNTER—The method of trading stocks not listed on a national or regional exchange.

PAPER PROFIT—An unrealized profit on a security still held.

PAR—In the case of a common stock, par means a dollar amount assigned to the share by the company's charter.

In the case of bonds, it means the figure at which interest is calculated.

PARTICIPATING INSURANCE—Insurance on which the policyholder receives reimbursement in the form of dividends reflecting the difference between the premium charged and the company's actual expenses.

PARTICIPATING PREFERRED—A preferred stock that is entitled to its stated dividend, plus additional dividends based on the common stock dividend.

PERMANENT LIFE INSURANCE—A phrase used to cover any form of life insurance except term; generally insurance that accrues cash value, such as whole life or endowment.

POLICY—The printed document stating the terms of the insurance contract that is issued to the policyholder by the company.

POLICY LOAN—A loan made by an insurance company to a policyholder on the security of the cash value of his life insurance policy.

PORTFOLIO—Holdings of securities by an individual or an institution.

PREFERRED STOCK—A class of stock with a claim on company earnings before payment may be made on common stock. It has priority over common stock if the company is liquidated.

PREMIUM—The amount by which a bond may sell above its par value. In insurance, the payment a policyholder agrees to make for coverage.

PROBATE—The judicial procedure to determine that a certain document claimed to be a will of the decedent is in fact valid and properly executed.

PROSPECTUS—A circular that describes securities being offered for sale to the public.

REGISTERED REPRESENTATIVE—Current name for the older term, "customer's man;" also known as "broker."

REMAINDERMAN—The person designated in a trust agreement to receive the principal at termination of a trust.

RENEWABLE TERM INSURANCE—Insurance which can be renewed at the end of the term for a limited number of successive terms. The premiums increase at each renewal as the age of the insured increases.

REVIVAL—The reinstatement of a lapsed policy by the company upon receipt of evidence of insurability and payment of past due premiums with interest.

REVOCATION OF A WILL—An act by a person who has drawn a will indicating his intention that the will shall no longer be effective.

RIGHTS—When a company issues additional securities, it may give its stockholders an advance opportunity to buy the new securities in proportion to the number of shares each owns. The piece of paper representing this privilege is called a right.

SECURITY—Evidence of property ownership, such as a stock certificate or bond.

SERIAL BOND—A bond on which interest and principal are paid at stated periodic intervals.

SETTLEMENT OPTION—One of the ways in which a policyholder or beneficiary may choose to have policy proceeds paid.

SPLIT—The division of the outstanding shares of a corporation into a larger number of shares. A 2-for-1 split by a company with 1 million shares outstanding would result in 2 million shares outstanding.

STOCK DIVIDEND—A dividend paid in additional stock rather than cash.

STOCK LIFE INSURANCE COMPANY—A life insurance company owned by stockholders who elect a board to direct the company's management.

SURROGATE—The title sometimes given to the judge who presides in the court where estates of deceased persons are administered.

TENANTS IN COMMON—Persons who own separate shares of

the same property which, in event of death, pass to their heirs.

TERM INSURANCE—Insurance payable to a beneficiary at the death of the insured provided death occurs within a specified period, such as five or ten years, or before a specified age.

TESTAMENTARY TRUST—A type of trust set up in a will, which does not become effective until after the death of the will's maker.

TESTATOR—The person making a will. When it is a woman, the word "testatrix" is used.

TICKER—A machine that prints the prices and volume of security transactions within minutes after each trade on the floor.

TRUSTEE—The person who controls or manages a trust for the benefit of specified individuals or organizations.

TRUSTOR—The person who sets up a trust and transfers property to it.

UNDERWRITING—The process by which an insurance company decides whether, and on what basis, it will accept an application for insurance.

UNLISTED—A security not listed on a stock exchange.

WAIVER OF PREMIUM—A provision that under certain conditions a life insurance policy will be kept in full force by the company without further payment of premiums. It is used most often in the event of total and permanent disability.

WARRANT—A certificate giving the holder the right to purchase securities at a stipulated price.

WHOLE LIFE INSURANCE—Insurance payable to a beneficiary at the death of the insured whenever it occurs.

YIELD—The dividends or interest paid by a company, expressed as a percentage of the current price of its stock; or, if you own the security, a percentage of the price you originally paid; also known as "return."

Index